Ethiopia Calls

Sandi Bokovoy

WESTBOW
PRESS®
A DIVISION OF THOMAS NELSON
& ZONDERVAN

WestBow Press books may be ordered through booksellers or by contacting:

WestBow Press
A Division of Thomas Nelson & Zondervan
1663 Liberty Drive
Bloomington, IN 47403
www.westbowpress.com
844-714-3454

Interior Image Credit: Alex Bokovoy

Scripture taken from the King James Version of the Bible.

ISBN: 978-1-6642-4391-0 (sc)
ISBN: 978-1-6642-4392-7 (hc)
ISBN: 978-1-6642-4390-3 (e)

Library of Congress Control Number: 2021918018

Print information available on the last page.

WestBow Press rev. date: 2/16/2022

Preface

I wrote this book so that others could see how God leads in unusual ways. We were both from such diverse backgrounds, yet God chose to use us and take us on an adventure far beyond what either of us could ever have imagined. I share experiences from our personal faith journey that brought strength, encouragement, and hope to us in various ways. I hope that you, too, will find answers to the questions you may have. My prayer is that readers will be inspired to take a risk and follow wherever God calls them.

During our Ethiopia years, most of our children were shepherds in their youth, and so I leave you with the Bible text, 1 Peter 5:4, that became very special to us, "And when the chief Shepherd shall appear, ye shall receive a crown of glory that fadeth not away".

Introduction

This book tells the story of how a young couple, committed to God, had the opportunity to serve in the beautiful country of Ethiopia. They had only been married one year when they moved halfway across the world. The story starts with their time in Dessie, a mountainous province in the northern part of Ethiopia.

The story of their lives in Ethiopia shows readers that the undeniable challenges of mission work are dwarfed by the immense satisfaction of providing physical and spiritual help to those who need it the most. Their experiences are a reminder that with God, all things are possible.

Dedication

3 John 1:4 (KJV): "I have no greater joy than to hear that my children walk in truth."

To my children Alex Charles, Joanna Lynn and James Dean, I dedicate this book.

A blazing white streak shot across the dark night sky. A huge boom reverberated against the stone walls of our compound. Army tanks were rumbling down the city streets. What was happening to our beloved country of Ethiopia? So little communication on the radio as it was mostly playing only music. We could not understand the occasional bulletins on TV. It was Wednesday night, and we were preparing our clothes for our appointment with the king tomorrow afternoon at the palace. We had been told that there was a new curfew at 8:00 p.m. It appeared no one was on the streets but the revolutionaries.

We had been invited to have tea with his Majesty, Haile Selassie at 2:00 p.m. on Thursday at the palace. We had been told of the protocol of the palace and prepared our children for the visit. Fifteen-year-old Alex Charles (Chuck) and fourteen-year-old Joanna Lynn (Joni) would follow protocol, but 5½-year-old James Dean (Jimmy) was told to keep quiet and not say a word as we had no idea what he might say.

Della Hansen, the royal housekeeper, had arranged our private visit with the king. Alex had often spoken with him when he would come to our hospital to check on a patient. Once he had come to check on the welfare of a lady who had eight children and was going to have her leg amputated, and he was concerned about her surgery. He loved his people. He had attended the dedication of our new hospital in 1968. He was very grateful for what we had done for his people. Now we were leaving Ethiopia after calling Ethiopia home for eighteen years—first in Dessie rebuilding Taffari Makonnen Hospital as the only doctor and now in Addis Ababa. Alex had served as medical director of the Empress Zauditu Memorial Hospital in Addis Ababa for nine years.

We arrived at the palace and were escorted into the private family quarters. The king arrived and greeted each of us. During our visit, Alex presented him a book called *A Century of Miracles* (by Richard Utt, Pacific Press Publishing Association, Mountain View, California, 1963), telling of our mission work throughout the world. We enjoyed our visit with the king. As we were leaving, he put his arm around our little son and said to him, "Jimmy, you will come back to Ethiopia someday, won't you?" Jimmy looked up at him with his big blue eyes and did not say a word.

After we left, we asked Jimmy why he had not answered the king. He said, "Mother, you told me not to say a word!"

Little did we know that on the following Monday, the king would be taken prisoner. The country of Ethiopia would fall to a new government aligned with communism. Many individuals would lose their lives during this regime, and the Ethiopia that we knew would never be the same.

Thursday night would be our farewell party. The curfew was set for 8:00 p.m. Would anyone come? So many people came. We were thrilled to see many friends, former patients, and people throughout the city that we had known. They brought so many gifts that we will always treasure. The gifts included Ethiopian gold, silver, different kinds of pictures, and gifts that were made locally in Ethiopia.

On Thursday night we heard the disturbing news that the airport was closed! Early Friday morning, Alex called the airport, and it had been reopened! Our friends took us to the airport in time for our flight with our three children and our suitcases. At the last security check, we were told we did not have a visa to Kenya, which would be our first stop on our way back to the United States. We told them we would take a chance. We prayed the full forty-five-minute flight that we could get a visa in Kenya and not be turned back. When we arrived, the security officer said that Ethiopia was always forgetting the visa and gave us the needed visa. We were so thankful! We were so fortunate to leave when we did. Alex had asked to leave a little early; he was supposed to oversee other hospitals in the Afro-Mideast Division as he also served as medical director for the division. It became exceedingly difficult for the missionaries, and eventually all the overseas missionaries were asked to leave. Our hospital had five American doctors, who were replaced with twenty Cuban doctors. That government was later replaced, but the Ethiopia we knew was gone forever. Our hearts will forever be with the Ethiopians that we had grown to love, and though we may never see them again, we will never forget the years of our service in Ethiopia.

Our Ethiopian story begins. How did this story begin? It all began with a vacation in Seattle, Washington, in June 1954. Our friends Jerry and Laura Dill invited me to go with them on vacation. Finally, I said I would go if I could babysit their two-year-old so they could have some free time. After arriving at the home of Jerry's parents, we were enjoying the days of vacation when one Thursday, Jerry arranged for us to spend the day in Seattle with his friend Dr. Alex Bokovoy. We arrived at the Lake City Medical Dental Clinic where Alex was a partner. Jerry went in and came out with this very handsome young man to meet us. Alex loved living in Seattle with his work and all the outdoor activities that he enjoyed. He was so full of energy and ready for us to enjoy a tour of the city. We had dinner that evening on one of the lakes, and then he took us to Greenlake Church, where I was to play the organ. Evidently, Jerry had told him I had graduated from college with piano as my major instrument. I thought it strange but did not know at the time that he was an outstanding soloist. Apparently, I passed the test, and a month later he invited me to spend a weekend with his sister near Santa Barbara. Having returned to my studies at Loma Linda School of Nursing, he surprised me by coming down for a postgraduate course of ten days before Christmas. This was an excuse for ten extremely packed days of fabulous dates, ice skating, a seaplane ride to Catalina Island where a Myna bird could "talk"—and said, "I can talk, can you fly?"—as well as a dinner at Palm Springs and a night at the Hollywood Bowl to hear a world-famous pianist. He literally swept me off my feet! He promised if I would go steady with him for six weeks, he would send me a ticket to fly to Seattle and meet his widowed mother. When I arrived, he had a special place to propose, but instead he pulled off the road to a safe place and proposed. After I said yes, he pulled out his wallet to a calendar and said, "Set the date!" We chose May 8. We had met in June. The relationship was going so fast, and we were in different states. I wanted to be sure he was a Christian, so I thought of a question that would help me know the answer. When he came to Southern California I asked, "If our church asked you to go as a foreign missionary, would you go?" He thought for a minute and said, "I have never thought about it, but if I thought the Lord wanted me to go, I guess I would go." Even I thought this was probably a total impossibility.

We were married in Pasadena, California, with our families and friends. We had a beautiful southern wedding with the girls in hoop skirts and men in white formal dinner jackets. We spent a month's honeymoon in the Hawaiian Islands. We really did not know each other well, as we had only spent three weeks together during our courtship days. The first time we went to church in Kapaa, Hawaii, Alex asked if we could volunteer for the special music. I asked, "Do you sing?" He asked the pastor, who accepted our offer. Alex chose the hymn "Open My Eyes That I May See." I played the introduction and was so shocked to hear this beautiful voice that filled the church. His was a voice that would sing for a king and bring many blessings to people around the world.

Returning to Seattle, it was a busy time. I received my first driver's license. Alex's mother would be staying with us for six weeks. The weather was so unlike my home state, Texas, that I bought my first raincoat—so many new experiences. Alex introduced me to his architect, Fred Basseti, who had finished a plan to build a home for Alex on Lake Washington. We changed the plans as needed for a family. He let out the plans for bids. We were so excited! Alex had included an entertainment room with a built-in screen that could also be used for Bible studies so that we could tell others of our best friend, Jesus. We prayed, "Lord, this is what we plan to do, but if you have other plans for us, let us know within two weeks."

Not sure why we prayed this prayer, but in exactly five days we received this letter from the general conference of our church on the East Coast, saying, "It gives me a great deal of pleasure to be able to inform you that the General Conference Committee this morning took action passing on to you a call to rebuild a hospital in Ethiopia."

For a moment we looked at each other. We had been praying, "Thy will be done," but we had not expected these instructions. We knew it must be the Lord's will. We canceled our former plans and began preparations for answering the call. Alex had been asked to rebuild a hospital that had been destroyed during the Italian occupation of Ethiopia. It was in Dessie, Ethiopia, the north-central area of the country. It had been called "Taffari Makonnen Hospital," which was the name of the emperor before he became king. He was interested in having it restored and had given the mission the land for a building that could be part of the remodeling to start the program. Good news! He was also in the process of building two homes—one for the doctor and one for the nurse. God had provided us the perfect new home, not in Seattle but in the mountains of Ethiopia!

We had to tell our architect. He surprised us with the information that he had been chosen for a government position to be an architectural adviser to Italy and would be leaving shortly. He invited us to visit his family in Rome on our way to Ethiopia. This was a unique opportunity to be guided by an architect in Rome, which we thoroughly enjoyed.

Thoughts raced through our minds. *What would we need to take with us? What would the country be like? What would it be like to be a missionary?*

We began making lists. Alex got out the atlas and showed me where Ethiopia was located. My geography was poor. It is in the northeastern part of Africa.

We purchased a canopy bed, which would save us from hordes of flying termites in the years to come, an old-fashioned Maytag washing machine, a pink refrigerator, a stove that was part electric and part wood, two carpet remnants, and bolts of unbleached muslin. We also included a sofa and two chairs. We were allowed extra baggage, as we were setting up a new area, and we needed also to take medical supplies. Alex bought lots of balls for different athletic games, as he enjoyed all kinds of games. He had played hockey for the US Air Force when he was in the army stationed in Germany. Then the days of packing and farewells ended. Our home church in Seattle had a special program to dedicate us for the mission work that the Lord had chosen for us. Pastor Fenton Froom of Greenlake Church led this service.

Dedication at Greenlake Church by Pastor Fenton Froom

This was the beginning of having to tell our wonderful friends farewell and not realizing that this would become all too frequent in the years ahead.

Soon it was time to leave. We left my parents at Memphis, Tennessee, and rode by train to Montreal, Canada. So hard for our parents to say goodbye as I was an only child, and Alex was the only son of his widowed mother. They are the ones who make the sacrifice. Alex's mother was seventy years old and did not know if she would live to see him again. She said she had dedicated him at birth, and if this were the plan of service the Lord had chosen for him, she would accept His will and would continue to pray for him. Alex's mother and sister were with us in Montreal as we boarded the RMS Ivernia on August 10, 1956.

We arrived in Liverpool, England, on August 21. We took

the train to London where we were met by friends. Alex attended the school of tropical medicine for a short time before we left for Germany. We went to several surgical places to purchase surgical instruments for our hospital. We rented a car and visited France, Austria, Switzerland, and back to Germany where we began our flight to Ethiopia.

Finally, on our way, our plane landed in Cairo, Egypt; Sudan; and Massawa, Ethiopia. We thought Egypt hot, Sudan hotter, and Ethiopia hottest! We were flying over Ethiopia and saw beautiful country—Lake Tana, high mountains, and a land covered in green velvet. Ethiopia is where the Blue Nile begins. Alex said, "This is a country I am going to like!" Happily surprised, we landed at the Addis Ababa Airport in Ethiopia at eight thousand feet, and the air was delightfully cool! Daytime temperatures were about seventy degrees all year round as it is located about ten degrees north of the equator.

We arrived on Tuesday and were taken to Dessie by Land Rover on Sunday. We had completed our registrations and licenses in Addis Ababa and had purchased basic supplies. We realized that we were now missionaries after our rugged, eleven-hour trip to Dessie. On the way we had seen a jackal, a hyena, and a family of baboons for which we had to stop the car as they passed over before us. The scenery was ever changing and so beautiful! We had passed through an area of the Rift Valley, climbed a twelve-thousand-foot mountain pass—Debra Sina—and back down to sea level and back up a winding road where we counted 140 almost complete switchbacks to the town of Dessie. Then we rumbled down a road below the town to a beautiful green field with a large white building on it. The grand climax came when we arrived at the gate to our mission compound.

Welcome greeting sign

Across the entrance gate was a huge sign, wreathed with tropical flowers with the words "Welcome to our Doctor." One European nurse, Ruth Boberg and about fifteen Ethiopian workers greeted us. Over and over, they said, "We have waited for a doctor so long, so long."

The first days were busy ones. First a part of the large building was to be made into an adequate operating area for surgery. Before it was completed, Alex had to do major surgery in one of the rooms. It was a splenectomy—the removal of a five-pound spleen. The only anesthetic available was ether or a spinal anesthetic. Generally, Alex had an Ethiopian nurse to assist him.

We also began to study the Amharic language with its 234 symbols and changing nouns, along with verbs that changed based on which person or persons you were talking with. Beautiful language but most difficult to pronounce!

Our new house would not be completed for about six weeks, so we were to stay in a European-type house in the town. The window openings did not have glass but were covered with wooden shutters that could be locked. We had no furniture of our own except a small wooden music box table that we had purchased in Rome, which was by the bed the hospital had provided. The bed was a Swedish style with the legs about a foot under the bed instead of on the corner. One night we heard the wooden shutters rattling, and brave Alex decided to check the noise. We had been told that thieves were in the area. He crawled over to my side of the bed, which caused the bed to flip, knocking the table over, which began to sing loud and clear, "O Sole Mio"! We could not contain our laughter, and we heard no more of the thief.

Food was a problem as we would have to depend on a garden. We were able to buy carrots and lentils. The Ethiopians' food consists of a crepe-like bread about twelve to eighteen inches around called injera, made of teff grain. It is very nutritious, as it is one of the highest protein grains in the world. Generally, it is eaten with a spice-filled legume stew that is delicious. Animals are their wealth, so meat is seldom eaten except for weddings, funerals, and special holidays. Therefore, we were able to buy lentils and carrots. For almost six weeks, we had lentils and carrots, and carrots and lentils, until we were ready for something else! I looked in my manual for my pressure cooker and decided I would make a bread pudding. It turned out perfect, and I set it on the counter awaiting my husband's return for lunch, forgetting that the windows had no glass and that the shutters were open to let in light. Alex was delayed at the hospital, and when he arrived, I brought him into the kitchen to see my surprise. It was a real surprise as where the pudding had been, now there was a Garfield-type cat, and not a crumb remained!

We were able to move into our house after about six weeks.

It was brick, and the floors were beautiful wood parquet. We had a large fireplace in the living room that was open to the dining room. There were three bedrooms, a large kitchen with a pantry, and a bathroom with a wood-burning hot-water heater.

A large wood stove was installed. Unfortunately, when the chimney was placed, the ceiling was not correctly insulated. One morning, Alex had gone to the hospital, and I went into the kitchen and saw that the ceiling was on fire. I ran to the hospital, meeting people on the way, and I would say, "My house is on fire," and they would smile and greet me. If only I knew the language. Arriving at the hospital, the translator for Alex saw me. I said, "My house is on fire!" He outran me and was able to put out the fire!

From the day we arrived, Alex immediately began to see patients—and what an array of medical problems. There were long-term ulcers, malaria, tuberculosis, unhealed wounds, stomach problems, and gunshot wounds. A judge came from seventy-five miles away to see the *hakim* as they called a doctor.

One day we drove to Baiti, a local Danakil market where hundreds came to barter for food, animals, and local products. We saw grass mats, spices, grains, cloth, sandals, and hand-woven clothing. There were little donkeys, each with a cross on its back, which had the legend it was the kind of donkey Mary rode with baby Jesus. There were one-hump camels that can carry five hundred pounds and are taught by the women to kneel and stand. The babies are adorable, but the adults have difficult dispositions. An elderly woman came to us and said, "Why is this foreigner here?" Our translator said, "He is a doctor," and she said, "What is a doctor?" and our translator told her that he was someone to make sick people well. She said, "I have fifty cents. Can he make me well?" The needs were so great. What could we do?

Peter Myheer with Sandi at the Bati Market

About a week after we had arrived, we received an invitation for tea with the crown prince and princess at their palace in Dessie. The prince oversaw this province. We were welcomed by attendants in palace uniforms and were taken to the blue room of the palace where we met the crown prince and princess. We were introduced and given seats by a small table where we were to be served. It was to be an informal visit about our work rebuilding the hospital. Alex told them of our plans, and the prince indicated they would do all they could to help us. They discussed the repairing of the road to the mission and would help to clean off the area of the compound. Then we were served hot chocolate, crackers with various spreads, and a delicious Boston cream cake. My husband shocked us all by asking the princess if she had baked the cake. She graciously answered that she had baked the cake! Before we departed, they gave us a case of grapes from Greece. This was a special treat!

About three months after our arrival, we went back to Addis Ababa and purchased our Land Rover. We got all the supplies of food that we could possibly pack into the car. Our eight-thousand-pound shipment had arrived, and we arranged for trucks to haul all of it to Dessie. When we unpacked out shipment, only one lid and one glass had been broken! On our trip back, we saw our first leopard as it was chasing a baboon on the mountain road. There were lots of monkeys, and we even saw a hyena at sundown. The last hour of our trip we began the long drive up the mountain to Dessie with its 140 switchbacks.

Dessie bus and a few of the 140 switchbacks

We would have to drive very carefully. On another trip later we saw a bus that had fallen off the road. The engine was several yards below what was left of the bus. The mountains reached up above our compound, and in the rainy seasons, they would be covered in green foliage so that it almost looked like velvet. It was so beautiful. Now Dessie would be home. We loved the Ethiopians that we had met. God had chosen this spot for our service to Him, and we were most blessed!

Three mission homes framed by the Dessie landscape

We had been promised a thirteenth Sabbath offering from our world church, which at the time was worth about thirty-five thousand Ethiopian dollars. We had also been promised a person to be in charge of the project. The man chosen by our mission headquarters was a talented man by the name of Hugo Palm from Sweden. He and his family had already served a five-year term in another part of Ethiopia. They arrived on Thursday—Pastor

Palm and Mrs. Palm with two adorable daughters, nine-year-old Anette and three-year-old Vivian. Saturday night, sometime after midnight, Mrs. Palm banged on our bedroom window, awaking us to hear that Vivian had a temperature of 106. Alex ran to the hospital and quickly drew blood for a slide that revealed Vivian had the deadliest form of malaria, Falciparum, which can affect the brain. He knew what medicine she needed, and the hospital had the medicine on hand. She immediately went into a convulsion, and he held her under a stream of cold mountain water in the tub and began working with her all night. She had one more convulsion and then slowly began to improve. When she awoke, she was holding Alex's hand and exclaimed, "You aren't my daddy!" We were all so thrilled to hear her speak as we had been constantly praying that the Lord would save her.

Vivian with Bambi in our garden

We had heard of another child in an area of Africa who had recently died of the same type of malaria.

Now it was almost Christmas, and half of the building had been made into a laboratory room, an X-ray room, a surgery room, two patient wards, and a reception area. The old army surgical table had collapsed on Alex's arm when he was delivering a baby, and he had to call for help to save them. We were desperately in need of equipment.

A new chapter begins. A verse in the Bible says, "Faithful is He that calleth you, who also will do it." (1 Thessalonians 5:24 KJV). Amazingly, we received a letter from a former professor and a physician, Dr. Knott from Seattle. He explained that he had heard Alex had gotten married and wished he could have met us before we left for the mission field. He was interested in our mission and wondered if there was anything we needed. Although Alex immediately wrote back, it would take about a month before Dr. Knott would receive the letter. Alex wrote back immediately saying that we needed a surgical table, a surgical light, an X-ray machine, and a generator to operate it all. Dr. Knott wrote back asking how much it would cost and where would be the best place to purchase the equipment. Alex estimated it would cost $12,000 US and all could be purchased in Germany. In the next letter was a cashier's check for $15,000. We told our mission family and had a special service to thank the Lord for answered prayer for the much-needed equipment. We wrote a deeply grateful letter to Dr. Knott thanking him for his generous gift. His wife wrote that the letter arrived the day of his funeral! She told us that the gift had made her husband happier than anything he had ever done. A few weeks later, the equipment arrived in perfect condition, and then our hospital was fully equipped and ready to open its doors. God had provided what we needed exactly when we needed it!

We learned that the people were extremely afraid of having

surgery and would not come to the hospital unless they were ready to die. During the first few weeks we were there, the only surgery Alex performed was an emergency splenectomy.

Then one night a man with a gun was chasing another man who he believed had been cheating with his wife. He shot at the man, but the bullet entered a hut and went through a man who was sitting inside! It entered his back and exited through his abdomen. His friends carried him to our hospital for surgery. The surgery went well, and the good news of his success quickly went throughout the area that the hospital could make sick people well. We were so thankful that God was blessing the hands of the surgeon, the hospital nurses, and the other hospital workers. The next surgical patient was a twenty-seven-year-old man who had been watching the family garden. Usually this was done by younger boys. He was using a slingshot to send out rocks to scare away the baboons. He was high in a tree when while slinging the sling high and above his head, he lost his footing and became unbalanced and fell through the tree. He impaled himself on a branch and tore open his abdomen, causing his intestines and other organs to spill outside of his body. Since he lived in a valley that was at sea level, below the Dessie mountains, it was a long way up to hospital in Dessie, over eight thousand feet above sea level. His relatives picked him up and put him in a wheelbarrow. There were no cars in his area. They covered him with a shemma cloth, putting a washbasin on top to hold his insides, and pushed him up the winding curves of the mountain road to our hospital in Dessie. Unfortunately, they arrived at night. We had never had a patient at night, so the night guard would not let them in. He had to wait for daylight. The guard never made that mistake again. Alex was able to flush out the rocks and leaves with gallons of saline solution and stitched him back together. Amazingly he recovered and became a worker at our hospital. God had performed another miracle. He was such a happy young man and later gave his heart to the Lord. He changed his name to Aragow Bokovoy! He was a Moslem and later became a Christian, marrying a Moslem who had become a Christian. They had two little boys who attended our Christian school.

When we arrived in Ethiopia, life expectancy there was only thirty-five years! Alex knew that immunization of the children would be necessary. Unfortunately, we had a limited number of vaccines, so we began by immunizing our hospital workers. We heard that many children died of smallpox. Our maintenance worker, Gibrab, had many scars from smallpox, but he had survived. It was the custom of the people, in their large huts, to bring their livestock in at night for protection. A typhus epidemic broke out in a nearby rural area, and many of our workers became ill. The typhus bacteria can be carried by fleas, lice, and mites living on animals. The workers lived in various places, many with poor accommodations with dirt floors and because of the shared surroundings with animals, the workers become ill. We had to do something as quickly as possible. We had a few funds on hand that we could use for building. Alex decided to build a long dormitory building for our single male workers so they could have better health. The building was made of mud and straw; all the local buildings were made in this manner. The building was whitewashed and looked nice. It had a cement floor. In addition, we built a school on the compound so that the workers could learn and be better prepared for their work. These young adult men would all begin in the first grade and progress as fast as they could.

The local typhus epidemic was widespread, and the government contacted our hospital to immunize twelve villages. Alex took a couple of workers and went to each of these villages giving as many immunizations as possible. The dreaded plague had reached epidemic proportions. Two policemen stood at the door as the people came in for their "morphia," as they called it. Two more policemen tried to control the crowd outside as the people were pushing and shoving trying to get in before the medicine would be finished. By noon, the medicine was gone, and he told them another worker would bring medicine within two days. Medicine for the vaccinations came from Addis Ababa, the capital city. He also visited those that were sick. As he left the last village, a man began to chase the car. He wanted an immunization, but sadly all the medicine was gone. They realized that without the medicine, they could die. A story was told to Alex at one of the villages. A family had died from typhus, except for the father, who was extremely ill. A thief came in to steal. The man asked for a drink of water, and as the thief gave him a drink, the man shot the thief. The next morning, the man was dead from the typhus, and the thief who had been shot was lying across the bed.

Peter Myrreh and the Danakils. One morning about eleven o'clock a, a hospital worker came to our home and brought a note for me that Alex had written: "I am bringing home a Norwegian fellow to have lunch with us today." This became the usual as foreigners often came to the hospital compound when they needed help in Dessie. As a new bride, my husband knew to warn me. I set another plate on the table and expanded the menu. I had no idea that this would be a life-changing moment. About one o'clock they arrived. Alex always asked a blessing on our food to share our thankfulness, but this time Alex asked our visitor to pray. Surprisingly, he prayed a beautiful prayer, and Alex asked, "Would you by chance be a Seventh-day Adventist?" He smiled and nodded yes. We discovered that he had been one of our earliest missionaries in Ethiopia. His name was Peter Myrreh, and he was from Norway. He held us spellbound as he told of his many years living in Ethiopia. He had come in 1931. He had traveled throughout Ethiopia, collecting plants and taking wood samples from many kinds of trees. He could speak and write more than twenty-four languages. He had written a Hebrew lexicon that was used in schools. He was a friend of the emperor. (Some years later, the king was on the platform at his funeral.) He had come to Dessie on a personal mission. He had been living with the Danakil tribe, and they were in a crisis as the Esau tribe had stolen eight thousand of their camels, and the tribe lives primarily on camel milk. They were facing starvation. He was on his way to Addis Ababa to obtain powdered milk for this nomadic tribe from the World Health Organization (WHO). The Danakil tribe was considered the most feared and warlike tribe in Ethiopia. Very few foreigners had ever entered the area of this tribe. He told Alex of the great need for this tribe to have medical help as there was no help in the deserts where they roamed. Because of Peter living as a Danakil and helping this tribe, he had won their trust. He lived like them and ate and dressed like them. He had also helped with a school. He had learned their language and was even now making it into a written language. He asked Alex if he would be interested in helping them. He would have to come down to the desert, and he would arrange for him to visit the villages along the Awash River. This Peter would do when he returned from his trip to Addis Ababa.

A few months later, it was arranged for Alex to go to Ascita with Peter. He was able to make the trip in our Land Rover, leaving the mountains to follow an almost indistinguishable path across the desert. On the road he saw zebras, gazelles, ostrich (that sometimes outran their car), strings of camels, and lots of large birds as well as other smaller beautiful birds. When he arrived, the sultan was shooting bottles off a fence with a few warriors. Alex came to them, and they handed him a gun and told him to shoot. This was not something Alex had ever done. He took the gun and shot, and the bullet shattered the bottle! The sultan was impressed and began to talk through two translators to him. He told Alex that he would provide forty armed guards to go with him on camels to the villages by the river. Alex could choose to ride a donkey or a camel. He made the mistake of choosing the camel and walked the last sixteen miles! It was an unforgettable trip out of the Arabian nights. The guards were extremely helpful, and Alex went from village to village.

The sultan with Alex

The leader of the Danakil warriors

Alex with Ali Abraham, the sultan's aide-de-camp

Guards for the journey

In one village, everyone had eye infections. Alex was able to treat them, and when they returned a couple weeks later, all were well and so thankful. In another village, everyone had tuberculosis, so there was little he could do to help. Many people had lost a hand or foot because of the crocodiles. The scenery along the river was so beautiful—many tropical trees were in bloom, gorgeous birds, and lots of monkeys too. At the end of the Awash River was an oasis of Edenic beauty that Alex took pictures of with weaver birds and other beautiful trees. The river was so muddy that if you put your hand in it, you could not see your hand six inches below. This was the only water source for the Danakils. They kept clean in this environment. Years later, another missionary doctor filled in for Alex. As he talked with the Danakils, they kept backing away from him. The doctor asked the translator if they were afraid of him, and the translator said, "No, you smell so bad." Both men and women wore a cotton wraparound skirt with lots of jewelry. The men were heavily armed with a curved sword at their waist, a walking stick that had a two-edged sword within on their shoulders, and a rifle with lots of cartridges across their chest. Alex would never be the same.

This was the beginning of a wonderful friendship with the sultan and the tribe. They were a very handsome tribe. The Danakil tribe had become his extended family. Years later when a Danakil would come to our hospital, the workers would tell him, "Your relative is here."

Shortly after the trip, the sultan sent his Land Rover with an older Danakil patient from the desert to our hospital. He had been in a serious fight. He had a real needle that a younger fellow wanted, and when the older fellow would not give it to him, the younger fellow threw his curved sword and almost cut the man's knee in half. Alex took him into surgery and repaired his knee and leg. He put a cast on it so it would heal properly. He seemed to do well, but a couple days after the surgery, he wanted to go home as our hospital did not have the food he was used to having. He told a hospital worker that he was ready to leave, so they called the doctor. Alex told him that he should stay longer, but the fellow said, "If you do not let me leave today, I will cut every patient's throat in the morning."

Needless to say, he was immediately discharged. A few months later when Alex visited the tribe, this man came to him; the cast was gone, he walked without a limp, and he brought Alex a goat as a gift to thank him. He is one of the patients Alex would never forget. We later heard that the Danakil patient had killed the man who had almost cut his knee in two.

Alex arranged to go to Ascita and hold a clinic about every six weeks. It was not unusual to see one hundred to two hundred patients in one day.

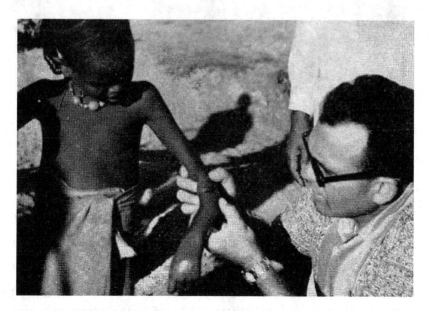

Alex examining small girl

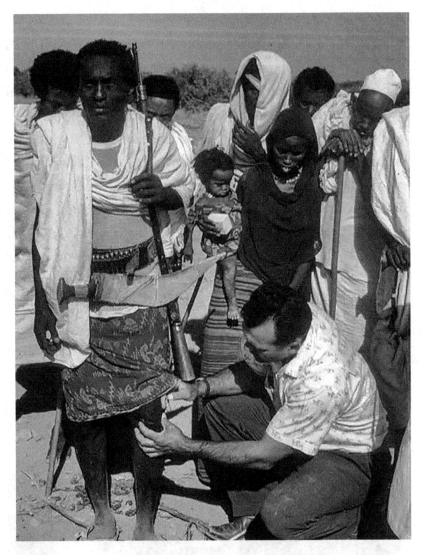

Checking Danakil man's healed knee

The Danakils are nomadic and travel throughout the desert. They carry everything they need on their camels. They have large straw mats that can be put together to make a little "room." One young couple were traveling, and when it became evening, they stopped and put up their little room. After their long, tiresome journey, they made their bed and quickly went to sleep They put their little baby girl, who was less than a year old, between them. During the night, a hyena stealthily crept in and took the baby by the head, and the baby cried out. The father took his stick and was able to hit the hyena before it had the baby through the door. The hyena dropped the baby, but she had a terrible laceration across her cheek under the eye. They were able to get to our clinic the next day, and God had brought Alex there just when he was needed. Alex was able to do the needed surgery and told them to come back later so he could do some plastic surgery on the little girl, but we never saw them again.

The emperor also sent word that he was giving us an airplane hangar building. We were able to connect it onto the end of the hospital. It was a real blessing. It provided a chapel on one end and a kitchen, dining area, and apartment for hospital workers temporarily on the other end.

Gift of the airplane hangar being added to the hospital

The hospital was becoming a reality. We would be the only well-equipped hospital in an area of two million people. Incidentally, Alex would be the only doctor as well.

The language barrier created its own problems. Alex ordered a month's course of treatment for a patient that included 120 pills. Soon the patient came back; he had taken all the pills in three days. Unfortunately, we saw evidence of the local medicine man as well. When a child has a fever, the parents will pull a tooth and keep on pulling teeth as well. When a baby is born, sometimes the parents will cut off the uvula, the little tag that hangs down in the middle of the throat.

During the years we were in Ethiopia, we were told that 96 percent of the population were farmers. We could understand that, as food was a priority. They planted teff, which was a millet-type grain for bread, and legumes and spices for making their daily hot stew. Breakfast consisted of barley tea. The only meal was in the evening of *injera* and *wat*, which usually was a stew made from vegetables or legumes. A visiting professor from Loma Linda University told us that teff was one of the most nutritious grains in the world. One of Alex's first priorities was to plant a garden. His mother, an experienced gardener, sent him all kinds of vegetable seeds as well as small berry plants. The soil was so fertile that it grew everything we put in it. Those first few weeks that we had lived on lentils and carrots gave us the motivation we needed for a garden. Alex hired a young man to help with the garden, and soon we had plants growing with the promise of a variety of vegetables. Then one sunny day we noticed it was becoming dark in the middle of the day. When we went outside, a dark cloud from the horizon was reaching in all directions, and soon it was above our heads.

The gardener yelled, "Locusts." Millions were fast approaching! He told us to make lots of noise and use whatever we could find to keep them from landing on our garden. We banged on pans and used long clothes to scare them away. It did help, but many of our small green plants were devoured. The garden was replanted, and in a short time, we began to harvest our first vegetables.

A few weeks later, we were introduced to another insect. One morning we noticed large black ants, which we found out later were called driver ants, coming into our house—not just a few but hundreds. We were desperately trying to figure out how to kill them when our house worker said, "No, you move out and let them have the house. They will go through the house for several hours and nothing living will be left."

He was right. They were better than any exterminator. No spiders, mice, or anything would survive. Sometime later we were told of a missionary who heard her baby crying in the night. She thought she would let him cry, but he continued, and when she went to him, the ants had swarmed his bed and would have killed him.

One day on the way to the capital, Addis Ababa, a huge black stripe was across the road. We stopped to see what it was. The driver ants are about an inch long and there were hundreds marching four and five abreast while other ants were standing as sentinels on each side of the line to keep them in order. Unfortunately, we could not wait and drove over them, and we could see them reassemble and continue their journey.

The third insect we encountered about a year after being in our new house was termites. We awoke one morning to have our bedroom filled with flying termites. They had come up from the wood floor but only seemed to want to get out and fly away. We were happy they left on their own accord.

Homemade medicine and the "evil eye." The homemade medicines they sometimes use are powerful enough to eat through the flesh, leaving large holes in the cheek. You can see the gums and teeth inside. They did not use sterile technique during the surgery they performed on each other, and infection would often develop. As a last resort, the victims were brought to the hospital. Often the children had "charms" tied around their necks to keep them safe from the "evil eye."

One night a patient was brought to our hospital that had been shot four times in the abdomen by *shiftas* (bandits). His condition required two major surgeries, and after he had been in the hospital several days, he was well on his way to recovery. Alex spoke with him, and he was so thankful to be alive that he had decided to stay and work at the hospital. He became a Christian and a good worker. The patient admission fee was fifty cents if they could afford it, but longtime patients could work for a while to help the hospital. The shooting was not an unusual occurrence. A few nights later a shot rang out, and then three shots in succession. A man had been killed across the street from our mission compound.

Special pet deer. About three months after our arrival, a patient brought us a fluffy little *Madoqua*, or dik-dik—a small antelope. We fed him by bottle, and he thrived. How much we enjoyed him! He could run like the wind but would come to us and loved to be petted. He eventually ate like a goat. He found a small cereal package and ate box and all. About six weeks later another friend brought us another little antelope, and we named him Bunky. During rainy season, the storms came with thunder and lightning at our altitude; it seemed we were inside the storm. One afternoon during a hailstorm, we heard a terrible cry. Alex, forgetting his shoes, ran out to the deer pen, but he was too late. Three wild dogs had jumped over the fence, and one had Bunky in his mouth. Alex had picked up a piece of wood and was able to hit the dog, who dropped Bunky, but the left hip and leg had been torn off. Nothing we could do but cry for our little friend. However, soon, another little deer-like animal was given to us, a *sesa*. The cord was still attached. It was about eight inches tall and ten inches long. He looked like a cartoon with ears like butterflies and Cleopatra eyes. He bounced when he walked and drank his milk from a bottle like a suction machine. These little animals brought us much joy.

Water. One of the most important needs for the hospital was a consistent water supply. Our maintenance man had found a large three-thousand-gallon tank, which he put on a scaffold so it could contain the rainwater during the rainy season and add to our supply. The town had a water system, but if an important man had a wedding, funeral, or other celebration, the water would be turned off in our area and given to whoever had arranged for it. This left us with no water. The first time this happened, Alex and Hugo went to the municipality and wanted to know why our hospital did not have water and was told of the problem. He explained that our hospital could not operate without water and pleaded for water to be returned to us.

Eventually the water returned. Then we heard the other side of Dessie began to complain about their lack of water. Shortly after this, we had a couple of Americans come to our hospital for medical help. Alex found out that they were well drillers from Oklahoma. He explained to them our lack of water problem. As they were working for the US government, they were not sure they could help us, but seeing our need, they decided to drill us a well on our property! The well was drilled, and pure water came gushing out. We were all so excited. God had answered another prayer!

Adventures of living in Africa. It took us several months to get used to our new country. There was water to boil and filter for drinking, vegetables to chlorinate, a wood stove that continually ran out of wood, and electricity from 6:00 to 10:00 p.m. We desperately needed a garden, and fortunately Alex was a master gardener. He soon had a supermarket garden in place. We were told that there were fourteen feet of topsoil in the mountains, and everything seemed to grow with little effort. The soil was so fertile that everything Alex had planted grew. He had to hire a helper, as visitors came day and night. We found an eighteen-inch porcupine quill one morning. Alex attempted to make a trap to catch him, but the porcupine chewed his way out. I heard a noise one morning in the garden and stepped out of the kitchen to immediately be grabbed in a hug by a baboon. He was almost as tall as I, as I am five feet two. The gardener was chasing him, and he was looking for help. Fortunately, when he saw the gardener coming around the house, he let go and ran away.

The beauty of the mountain peaks surrounding our plateau was like lush green velvet. There were lots of wildflowers. We sometimes took a picnic on the side of the mountain, and the monkeys seemed to enjoy watching us as much as we enjoyed watching them. We could not have been living in a more beautiful country. We were in Africa, and wild animals were in our area also. One moonlight night, I was walking down the white gravel path that led from the hospital to our house, and suddenly I literally ran into a hyena. I frightened the hyena, and it frightened me, and I quickly ran to my house as fast as I could go.

Hyena in the town of Harar

There was no electricity, but the moon reflected on the white gravel path so I could find my way home. Another night we heard what sounded like a child crying in the pasture below our house. Alex took his powerful flashlight and shined it toward the sound. There were eight pairs of eyes surrounding a hyena that had caught his leg in the wire fence, and they were obviously waiting for him to die so they could feast on their "friend." The most beautiful animal we saw was a Somali leopard the color of caramel. She was at the US agricultural center near Harar. Another time on our way to Addis we came around a corner and a leopard was chasing a baboon. The leopard jumped over a small cliff going down the mountain while the baboon ran up the mountain to freedom.

World War II's impact. We had heard stories of the World War II fighting of the Italians in Ethiopia and especially in Dessie by a former missionary, Dr. Stadin, from Sweden. Our Taffari Makonnen hospital had been marked on the roof with a huge red cross, but it was still bombed. They had to flee Dessie and go to Addis Ababa, and the war followed them. One evening, Dr. Stadin's wife was sleeping in her bed when a bullet passed through and killed her. Dr. Stadin told us that he had given the supreme sacrifice in his mission service when we met him in the States years later when we were on furlough. He encouraged us to continue the work he had started. However, we were also to see the remnants of war.

One day a car came to our hospital from Kombolcha, near sea level. There were few toys for the children in our area. A group of boys had been playing on a cement foundation that had been left since the war. One of the boys found a metal "ball." They were enjoying throwing it back and forth. Then one of the boys missed, so the boys all fell on the spot where it landed, and it exploded, as it was an old hand grenade. Two of the boys were killed immediately, the others had terrible wounds. They were brought to our hospital as soon as possible. Alex began to repair them. One of the boys would have to have his leg amputated. The father was standing in the hall crying, and the workers tried to comfort him. He told them he had two sons. One was born a cripple and now this son, who he had hoped would farm and take care of him in his old age, would also be a cripple. Alex and all tried to console him, but he was too distraught. He would hold his head in his hands and would continue to moan and cry. How we wished we could help him!

We had often wondered why this hospital in Dessie had been chosen for our work. We had been sent to reopen the Taffari Makonnen Hospital in Dessie. It was about 250 miles north of Addis Ababa. The name was the name of the emperor before he became king. Later we read the story of why this hospital was so important to him. The property had been a gift from the emperor in 1925 of $15,000. On the staff was Dr. George Bergman from the USA and nurse Adam Ali. On October 2, 1935, the Italians invaded Ethiopia from Eritrea. The hospital was then run by Dr. and Mrs. Adreas Stadin from California. Thanksgiving dinner, November 28, 1935, was special. Thanksgiving dinner, including pumpkin pie, was prepared by Mrs. Wells, a journalist; Mrs. Stadin, the doctor's wife; and nurse Mrs. Hovig for forty news journalists and hospital staff. Eighteen news organizations were represented and gave a gift of 200 thayers (Ethiopian dollars) to the hospital.

The Italians had entered Ethiopia from the north and were coming south to Addis Ababa. Dessie was about 250 miles from the capital. Apparently, the Italians had heard that the emperor was in Dessie. On December 6 and 7, the palace in Dessie and the hospital were bombed. Forty-one bombs were dropped on the hospital, which had been painted with large red crosses. An eyewitness account was published in *Reader's Digest* 329 (June 1936, pp 75–77) by Wynant Davis Hubbard, an America correspondent. The emperor himself was in Dessie with his eleven-year-old son, the duke of Harar. The palace was in flames, but the emperor's son was able to get out unharmed. The emperor immediately began directing his soldiers. He had no way to counterattack though he used a machine gun himself to try to fight the planes. Sixty patients were evacuated from the hospital, along with the journalist. He helped many of the injured who were brought to the hospital with burns and broken bones. Hundreds of patients came. The city became a no-man's-land with killing and looting. The next day, a Thanksgiving service was held for those who survived, and the emperor took part as well. He said, "You have received and cared for our sick and taught our people, but more than that, you have remembered that our trust is in God, and have not forgotten to pray to Him for us. We thank you." All the workers left, but the war followed them to Addis Ababa. The emperor left Ethiopia and went into exile in Europe. He sent a telegram to the United Nations about the attack on the hospital, but nothing was done. Now we knew why the emperor wanted this hospital restored, and we were honored to have been called to rebuild the Taffari Makonnen Hospital.

In 1952, the government asked the Seventh-day Adventist Church to receive the Dessie hospital again. On June 24, 1953, Dr. Bernarr Johnson and Pastor Eric Palm were able to receive seventy-four hundred square meters of property that had one big house on it in good repair that had been an army barracks. The former hospital land could not be returned, as the Italians had built a hotel there. Dr. Johnson and family stayed a year and a half and were called back to the hospital in Addis Ababa. Now we had been called to make the emperor's request be finished. The mission was to continue, and the hospital was restored.

When we first came, there had been many kinds of prejudice to overcome. The local medicine man was particularly good at setting broken bones, but his concoctions did little to heal diseases. He had circulated the rumor that the heart, liver, and kidneys taken from the patients were to be eaten. How could they believe such talk? Several months later, one day a man finally came to our hospital. He told the hospital worker he did not want to see the doctor. He insisted that he only needed an injection! The worker told him he would have to see the doctor to diagnose him so he would know how to treat him. After questioning him further, the local medicine man had told him he could not help him more and to go to the mission and get an injection. This was the years when penicillin was still new. We had the antibiotics, but some unscrupulous men were giving people injections of milk.

History of Christianity in Ethiopia. There was also prejudice that we faced as Christians. Almost two thousand years ago the gospel had come to Ethiopia. The Bible speaks of the Ethiopian eunuch who was reading the prophecies, and God sent Phillip to explain it to him. We also read in the Bible of the visit of the Queen of Sheba to King Solomon. Most of the kings had been of the Christian faith. We found an island near our mission where the monks could tell us why they kept the seventh-day Sabbath. It was kept for hundreds of years until the Sunday Sabbath was introduced by one of the later kings. Now Ethiopia was considered about half Moslem in our area. We were not allowed to hold religious services outside of our compound. However, Ethiopia was a country that was supposed to have religious freedom. Some members of our church were taken in northern Ethiopia and were beaten. They were then put in prison. Word was sent to Addis Ababa, and the emperor sent word again that these young people were to be released immediately.

Pastor Dessie Kassahun. Our own mission leader for our area was Pastor Dessie Kassahun. We were so thankful for him. He had been one of the first Ethiopian nationals to be sent for further education at Spicer College in India. He received his degree and was unable to return to Ethiopia as the Italians had taken over the country. He served in Kenya until the war was over and returned home to Ethiopia. For us, we were blessed that he spoke English fluently and became our teacher for us to learn Amharic. It is the most difficult language as it has 234 characters, and each symbol has seven versions. He had a lovely wife and four sons. He had to travel eight to ten days by mule through the mountains and valleys to visit the Tarna area where there were many church members. They were from the first converts of Sheik Zacharias. They were paying tithe as they wanted the Lord's blessings, so they were very faithful. As Pastor Dessie would preach and share the good news, he would then accept the tithe and bring it back to Dessie to take it on to the headquarters in Addis Ababa where it would be used to continue to spread the gospel. One day when he was coming home by donkey through the mountains, he looked at the long road and knew there was a shorter way, but he prayed and was impressed to go the longer way. He returned to Dessie and was told that shiftas, or robbers, had been waiting for him along the shorter route, and he was safe with all the tithe money. Surely the Lord was with him. It impressed us that the Lord was working among our Ethiopian workers, and we were all members of the family of God.

The story of Sheik Zacharias. The story of Sheik Zacharias must be told. He was a devout Muslim, and in 1891 during the month of Ramadan, he secluded himself in a wall stone house of prayer that he had constructed, and there he prayed for seven days. The Lord appeared to him in vision. From that time on, he was given a clear understanding of the Koran. Later another vision told him to harmonize the interpretations of the Old and New Testaments. From that moment on, he was given a third person to guide him in his diligent studies. He remained a Moslem for fifteen years and then led his hundreds of followers into Christianity. The only Christian church at that time was the Orthodox Coptic church. He disagreed with worshipping icons and statues, but the church accepted them anyway. However, he continued to study and found baptism should be by immersion, the seventh day was the Sabbath, and many other subjects that prepared the way for his new Christians to later become Seventh-day Adventists. He was accused and called before various government courts, but he was able to speak of the Koran and the Bible so well that he was not imprisoned. He was listened to by both Moslems and Christians. Yet there were some who wanted him to stop preaching and teaching. He finally was taken before the great King Menelik II of Ethiopia, and the king was so impressed that he issued a proclamation that Sheik Zacharias was free to go throughout the kingdom teaching Moslems as well. This was 1899, and as he now was authorized by the king, he was free to continue his travels throughout Ethiopia. There is documented proof of this man's story by Ato Truneh WoldeSelassie in his book, *Adventism in Ethiopia: The Incredible Saga of the Beginning and Progress of the Seventh Day Adventist Work in Ethiopia* (Truneh WoldeSelassie, 2005, self-published). Sheik Zacharias changed his name to Newaye Christos when he was baptized as a Christian. He had preached nineteen years as a Moslem before becoming a Christian. Even as a Moslem, he often said the words, "Thus saith the Lord." He had studied diligently and disagreed with the only Christian church in the area where he was baptized, and soon persecution began, and although he had never heard of a Seventh-day Adventist, he had studied himself into accepting baptism by immersion, the seventh-day

Sabbath, salvation, tithing, and many other principles followed by the church.

He had also been given instruction that one day a man would come that would lead them into more light. This man would be teaching with three translators. This exact thing happened in Asmara when his close friend, Aleka Motbainoe, attended Seventh-day Adventist Church and saw Pastor Ogbagzy, an Eritrean speaking in English with three translators. Pastor Ogbagzy was the first ordained pastor of the Seventh-day Adventist Church in Ethiopia. Aleka Motbainor returned home and told his village what he had learned, and the whole village accepted the new teachings, and ten other local villages also joined them. This was the beginning of the Seventh-day Adventist Church in that area.

Sharing Jesus with the children. A few weeks after we arrived, Alex and I agreed we would begin our Christian service. I would take the children, and he would teach the hospital workers and friends of the mission in an adult meeting. My first two children were boys: Nega was the son of a Christian hospital worker, and the other was Mohammed, son of a Moslem lady who oversaw the kitchen. They were both about ten years old. No one seemed to keep their actual birth date. The parents would just say they were born before or after the rains. My Mohammed was from the mountains extending above our hospital. There were many shepherd boys and girls keeping their parents' animals: sheep, goats, and a few cows. Mohammed loved to sing and was a soloist by nature. He also loved the programs and invited many of his Moslem friends to come, and soon we had twenty-five children coming regularly. One would stay with the animals while the others would come down the mountain, cross a small river, and go up to our plateau where the mission was located.

We had only three girls coming, Mulu, Dinknish, and Atenish. The months passed, and they learned to know about God, prayer, and exciting stories from the Bible. One day, early in the morning, I heard a knock on my door. I opened it, and there stood Mulu and Atenish; both had been crying. I finally was able to understand the problem. Atenish had come to our children's program and left her younger brother to watch the animals. A short while later her brother Getacho also came down the mountain to hear our program. When they returned up the mountain, they found the sheep and the goats, but their two cows were missing. The other children tried to help, but they could not be found.

When evening came, and Atenish took the animals home, her father asked, "Where are the cows?"

Atenish said, "We couldn't find them." The father closed the door with Atenish outside.

Atenish went to Mulu's house for the night. In Africa, people and animals are inside for the night. The girls had come to my house, and I told them that I would pray, and Hakim (doctor) would have the workers pray at the hospital morning worship. All day we prayed. That evening, just before the sun went down, we looked down the road near the mission and the two cows were going down the road to their house! No one was with them! God had sent his angels to keep the cows safe through the night and had brought them home safely! We had vacation Bible school the following summer and had sixty children, and each year after that would double our attendance. It was so much fun to watch the children learn much that would change their lives for the better. We chose three boys to send to our Christian boarding school, and today Nega is a medical doctor, and Mohammed, or Ayalew, as he is now called, has taught English to many that are not only in the work of the mission but have been part of the Ethiopian government.

Daily life. Every day seemed to have a different schedule. The hospital needed curtains for the ward rooms, so I was asked to make the curtains. We had brought bolts of heavy unbleached muslin, which was perfect for the drapes. I had little sewing experience, but as a kid I had been in 4-H club where we learned the basics for sewing, thankfully. I was able to make many curtains and cut out patterns for the workers' uniforms. We found blue gingham for the dresses that were to be worn with an apron. Obviously, the uniforms were based on my student nurses' uniforms. The men had a long jacket type shirt with white pants. At the time we were in Ethiopia, most of the men still wore white pants as their regular Ethiopian pants, which were designed like riding pants. A long white tunic went over the pants. Women wore beautiful white dresses with embroidery for dress occasions and a completely natural white cotton for daily wear. They only received new clothes at New Year's, so before the next year was over the clothes were quite worn. They washed them in the streams nearby, and there was a shrub with blossoms that acted like Clorox so they could stay white. They would lay them out on the pasture in the sunshine to dry.

Hikum and the Danakils. A call came to the hospital telling Alex to come to Ascita. Three of the chiefs had malaria, and Peter Myheer was also extremely ill. Alex left for Ascita and found the sultan in a room surrounded by men with American-made machine guns. He was invited in and immediately began to see patients. He saw seventy patients, including four of the sultan's wives and ten of his sons. He got back from Ascita in time to see a patient who had a bullet lodged in her intestine. She had been shot twenty-four hours before and already had infection. Alex did a colostomy on her, and she recovered well.

Nurses. Alex and I were asked to go to Addis Ababa and take part in the nurses' graduation. Alex was to sing, and I was to play the piano for the service. The Addis Ababa Empress Zauditu Memorial Hospital provided nurses for the main hospital in Addis Ababa and for the three other mission hospitals. There was a hospital in the north in Debra Tabor and a hospital in Gimbi in the west besides our hospital in the north-central area. Graduating nurses were asked to serve a year in one of our hospitals. We were first given a young nurse—Tehun—and later, as we grew, we received two nurses at a time well trained and a real blessing for us.

After arriving home, Alex had two patients who had to have a colostomy. One had been shot through her side. Both recovered well and had their colostomy repaired so they would be normal again.

Alex had brought back roses to plant in our garden, and that was the beginning of our beautiful landscape. Everything grew so well. One sunflower grew twelve feet tall! A swarm of bees decided to make our sunflowers their home, and we were able to find a man who could put them in his straw basket and take them away. We had many kinds of flowers as well as many delicious vegetables! So thankful that Alex was in charge of our garden and not me!

We had arrived in August; our first year was almost over, and we were able to open our new clinic in June. The clinic was in front of the hospital. There was an X-ray room, a lab room, a doctor's office with two examining rooms, and a reception area with two waiting rooms. Now we would really say we were ready for patients. One morning a young lady came in to have her first baby. She was from the Sudan Interior Mission, which worked with a leprosarium. I was so happy to have an American to share our thoughts with. She had her baby, and I made her meals the days she was in our hospital, so we became good friends. That was something good, as we shared our hospital with all denominations and felt we were working together for Jesus.

Daily life. The SIM mission brought us two heads of cabbage and twelve carrots! We have learned how important the "little rains" and the "big rains" are for food! Our garden grew so well when it had rain, but then the months between the rains could be very dry, and water must be carried if we wanted the vegetables to grow a little longer. We can understand the grumbling Israelites. However, we still had a few greens and beans growing. Now it was May and our second wedding anniversary. I would make a special dinner that night with what we had. At least I could bake a cake now in the wood stove and know it would be a good one. Baking powder cakes did not work so well in the high altitude, but soda cakes worked, and especially chiffon cakes raised out of their pans. Our special meal for visitors was to fire up the stove as hot as we could get it and bake pizza, and as the temperature dropped, I could put in brownies and have a delicious meal!

Alex was happy that he was busy with patients as our hospital reputation was growing. Every one of Alex's surgical patients were exceedingly difficult. They came when they thought there was no other hope. God is good, and they all lived!

One patient came in that had been shot more than twenty-four hours before and was already infected, but after surgery he did well. Another patient came in with a foot that looked like a claw. Alex did plastic surgery on him as infection from a thorn had eaten away part of his foot. He was able to help the man so that he was able to walk again.

Friends and food. We often had unexpected company as travelers need food and water. We had a pastor, Lester Rasmusson, and wife, Alice, from Washington State, arrive with five of the best-behaved children and stayed the weekend. Unfortunately, he bit into an ear of corn grown locally and lost a front tooth! When we did not have unexpected guests for the weekend, we enjoyed inviting our hospital workers two or three at a time. We served the local wat and injera for them. We had already learned to like their national food too. The interesting thing about it is how it is eaten. There is no need for a plate or utensils as they fold the crepe over in half and then again. The stew is placed on the bread, and the bread is broken off, and the stew is picked up by the bread.

Sewing. All the uniforms were completed by the end of June, and the hospital workers were so proud of them, as were we. The new clinic was officially opened, and many patients were waiting to get in the door. Our hospital now had twenty-five beds for patients. We were also sent two Ethiopian nurses from our training school in Addis Ababa; one would help in surgery and the other in the clinic. The first year was not quite over but we were making progress.

Then again no water for five days. We had to arrange for water to be carried in. The city had a three-inch pipe, and our pipe was a half-inch pipe to our hospital. We exchanged it for a three-quarter-inch pipe, which helped.

We had a little excitement. A swarm of bees landed on our tall sunflowers, and we quickly called someone who knew about bees. He was able to put the swarm in a large straw basket and take them to another area. Often, we had seen these baskets in trees but had not known that they were special for the bees, and the honey could be bought at the local market.

We had a fellow who would go to the local market and bargain for the food needed at the hospital, and he would give another fellow ten cents to help him carry the food back.

The Moslems will not eat any meat unless it is killed by a Moslem in a specific way. We were able to not have that problem with our food as we only served vegetarian food at our hospital, which is the usual Ethiopian food for the local people and very nutritious as we used a lot of legumes like lentils with their high protein and iron bread. Interestingly, our hospital was located next to the prison compound. Five times a day we could hear the gong from the prison calling the Moslems to prayer.

We also heard that a four-motor Constellation, the first that Ethiopian Airlines had received, caught fire while in flight. The pilot was able to land the plane, and all the passengers were safe, but the plane was destroyed.

Sad news, the emperor was in mourning. His son, the Duke of Harar, was killed in a car accident. He would not be able to attend any official programs for some time.

Rainy season. It was the rainy season then, and the lightning and thunder made it seem like we were surrounded. Pastor Dessie told us that many people are killed by lightning. We were at eight thousand feet, so it seemed we were inside the storm! Despite the rain, our twenty-five hospital beds were full, and we were anxious to complete the rooms for the next twenty-five beds. The patients may take several days walking to the hospital, or they may be brought by friends or relatives. Often the local medicines have been tried first, and our hospital was their last resort. Alex saw lots of infections and patients with bowels filled with gangrene. There had been a bad flu epidemic in the Middle East, and unfortunately it came to Ethiopia. Alex and I both had the flu, but it did not last long—only a few days—but then we were getting more patients with the flu.

Treasures from home and new friends. We had an American come to our hospital on his way home and left us with American Commissary articles that he did not need anymore. What a blessing! There was real sugar, Kraft cheese, three dozen bottles of root beer and three of cherry, and Fig Newtons—all so American!

We had a lovely lady come to our hospital from the SIM mission. This was her first baby, and she had an eight-pound baby naturally. She had met her husband in language school, so she did not have anything for a baby. She had made a little shirt out of the tail of her husband's undershirt, as there was no place to buy baby clothes, so our overseas ladies made baby clothes and items for her the best that we could. We became fast friends, but because of the distance of their mission compound, we seldom saw them. We drove to their mission a couple times, but the road was so bad that the speedometer on our Land Rover registered "0 kmh" as we went from pothole to pothole.

Our children's program grows. Our children's program was growing. We had gotten coloring books and crayons from Addis Ababa, which was something new for them. Recently we had forty-three children, mostly from the shepherd children from the mountains behind our mission. Then we planned a vacation Bible school during rainy season and had sixty children come for our first vacation Bible school. All the crafts were made from local material. We used the natural cotton for mats to color pictures on. We made pictures with seeds on sandpaper, and belts of small blocks of wood laced together. How I loved those children! They loved the Bible stories even though I had to use a translator. They loved to sing and always were so cooperative. It was a real joy to work with them.

Vacation Bible school in Dessie continues to grow

Learning Amharic (the Ethiopian language). The Amharic language was difficult for us since we did not get formal training. Still, we began to learn it to communicate and build relationships. We had two young people working for us. One young man, about fifteen years old, made our wood fires, to keep the wood stove in the kitchen going and to keep the fireplace burning, as there was no other heat in the house. Our hot water heater was a wood burning heater. The other young person was a girl, Allemnish, to help with the housework and laundry that was done outside, and the clothes were dried on the lines. I wanted her to take a day off, but she would come every day, and I would have to send her home on her "day off." There had not been a need for her to count the days except the day to come to church. One day our boy, Mamo, asked if I needed wood. I said yes and found out that I had just bought six donkey loads of wood. One donkey load was fifty cents and carried about fifty sticks of wood for the stove! After a few months, Allemnish went back to school, and Jerusalem helped me. Every time I said her name, I felt like singing the song "Jerusalem"! She was a lovely girl and later married a pastor. It was a great experience getting to teach her things that she could later use in her own life. At the beginning, she dried the dishes with the tablecloth, and so her learning began. I really needed help even though I loved to cook. Everything I did was so involved, whether boiling water, cleaning vegetables that had to be scrubbed and soaked in bleach water and then rinsed thoroughly, or doing the laundry. We paid them thirty dollars a month, which was the usual wage for that time. Mamo went to school at nights with the workers and worked for us all the years we were in Dessie.

We had been in Dessie a year now, and what a year! Alex felt he was right where he was meant to be. This had to be one of the places in the world where the needs of the people were greatest. They needed to be helped with their daily lives, to learn basic cleanliness to help them be healthy and to learn to read and write, and needed help medically and spiritually.

The Lord had blessed in so many ways. Our clinic was finished, and soon the hospital compound would be finished. The long Ethiopian "siesta" from 1:00 to 4:00 p.m. gave Alex a chance to get some physical activity. He was an athlete and had brought with us every ball that he could think of. He began playing volleyball with the hospital workers. Then the local high school boys noticed and came to play also. He enjoyed the time so very much making friends with the local people, which opened the way for some unusually good "bread on the waters." Several years later, we were returning from furlough with our three children and had new articles on which we would be charged customs entering the country. One of Alex's volleyball friends was now the director of customs and marked our suitcases with chalk and let us go through the airport without having to pay any customs.

Beauty during and after the rainy season. Nearing the end of the rainy season, the garden looks like a supermarket. Although the days were warm, the nights were getting colder, and by December the frost would finish the garden. Mohammed brought me the most beautiful flowers from the mountain, which had gold-colored flecks with rich red and brown colors inside. They grew tall like gladiolas. Ethiopia is one of the most beautiful countries in the world. The rains make the mountains look like green velvet in the distance.

Patient stories. More interesting patients were coming in. A man was driving down the mountain when his brakes failed. He stopped the car by running into the mountain. He went into shock, but when he was brought into the clinic, he had only broken one rib. Another man was driving when some people started throwing rocks at him. Unfortunately, he stopped and argued with them, and they beat him up. He came to the hospital to be helped. Another man came and said he was possessed by the devil. This is not unusual, as the witch doctor will put a "curse" on people, and they believe they will die. Alex called the chaplain to talk with them, and then he sometimes gave them a vitamin injection that made them feel hot, and they were thankful and felt the devil had left! He also did his first eye surgery, an entropion, where the eyelid turns inward and infects the eye. Each day was a new experience.

Just started dinner and Alex was called away for an accident patient. Three Eritrean policemen had been killed in the past month. The police were already at the hospital to keep watch on this Gala patient; they believed a Gala shifta (bandit) was involved. There were so many tribes, each with their own language and customs. Amharic and English are taught in the schools now, but Ethiopia is considered 96 percent illiterate at this time. Alex's translator spoke seven or eight languages, including Arabic and Italian as well as the local Amharic and Gala languages.

I cut out ten more dresser uniform jackets as our staff was growing. I had denim left from my slipcovers, so I was making little stuffed horses for all the workers' children for Christmas.

We had a thrill of a lifetime January 15, 1958! We were called from the American Embassy in Addis that a helicopter would be picking up a young secretary who had fallen from her horse in Lalabella. There is a tourist attraction of churches built of stone in the mountains that are so beautiful that they can be compared to the cathedrals in Europe. They were built during the time of the Crusades in the eleventh century. It was about an eight-day journey by mule from us. We were told to lay out a big white sheet where the helicopter could land and four smaller ones around it. Unfortunately, we were near a stream where the local ladies were doing their washing with their long white cloths called shemmas lying out in the sun to dry. However, the pilot was able to set the helicopter down, and hundreds of Ethiopians came to see it, flowing through the mission fence. Fifteen policemen were sent down to protect the plane that evening. Alex missed dinner with our guests as he was in the hospital sewing up the poor people that had come through the compound fence and had injured themselves. The next morning the pilot took us up for a short ride so Alex could photograph our hospital compound. We also saw a huge waterfall behind the mountain where we lived that we had never seen! There were only three helicopters in the country at that time. The pilot and men that came slept in our house that night, and because we could help the Ethiopian Airline (EAL) manager, he allowed the local Kombolcha airport to use our hospital from that time on. The publicity was good for our hospital. The patient was flown on to Addis and recovered.

Visit to Addis Ababa, the capital city of Ethiopia. We were asked to attend our mission annual meeting in Addis. We were told we had missionaries from forty different countries. Four doctors were from America, and one doctor was from Britain. At our evening meetings, Alex was asked to sing a special song every night. We did our grocery shopping at our Greek "uncles" store, as it was the only grocery store that carried the supplies we needed. They became particularly good friends from the time we got our supplies there until we lived in Addis Ababa, when they would give our children chocolate bars that cost $3.50 apiece!

Back home. We came home to a beautiful garden and were so good to be home. Ethiopia was home now in so many ways. Alex's first patient was brought in from the desert several hours away. She had been bleeding and had no blood pressure and a thready pulse. The husband refused surgery until almost too late. Alex had some war surplus transfusion bottles and was able to type some relatives and give her the needed blood. She had a ruptured fallopian tube, and after surgery she again began to bleed, so he had to go in a second time and was able to repair a second area of bleeding. She recovered and was good publicity for the hospital. Shortly after, a man came in with the bone sticking out of his leg, which required surgery. He had been driving a truckload of peppers over these tortuous roads, and his truck exploded. So thankful that our new X-ray was installed! Alex repaired his leg, and he was able to go home later. He was so thankful, as he had thought Alex was going to amputate his leg.

Our children's group at church was growing. We had sixty-five children that weekend. So exciting to teach them of Jesus, to pray, and to know that God is love. They believe that God has an "evil eye" and is watching them to discipline and not to love. We had a celebration for Easter. I made cinnamon rolls and huge bowls of popcorn. Then we had a piñata made from a brown paper bag full of candy. The children loved it and had probably the most candy they had ever had! Our VBS has grown from about twenty-five to more than one hundred.

The little rains come mostly at night, but I think little rains is a misnomer! Last night the thunder, lightning, and windstorm made us feel like we were in the middle to it. It even hailed! It came in sheets of rain. Good for the garden as the corn was shoulder high, with peas, string beans, and new potatoes on the way. No shop to buy, so happy for the garden for variety. Soon we would have been in the mission field a full year. How fast the time goes!

The man from Europe came to install the X-ray. Our hospital was now complete with the surgery table and surgery light in their proper place and a working generator. Our completed hospital had fifty-five beds.

Taffari Makonnen Hospital—front view

Taffari Makonnen Hospital—side view

Our Danish nurse, Ruth Boberg, would be leaving, and it was such a loss, as she spoke the language fluently and had been the leader in the hospital. We had our first case of tetanus. The man said he did not want to spend the money for care and came in too late; despite giving him all the antitoxin we had, he died. It is so difficult to get the people to understand that they must come before it is too late. Later there were other patients that we were able to save with tetanus.

More patient stories. A father brought in his daughter. He had carried her for a long way as there were no cars in his area. She was almost lifeless, and my husband began to see if he could find the cause of her illness. He examined her and yet was not able to find the cause, so he began again. They opened her mouth, and he noticed something in the back of her throat behind the uvula. After a closer examination, he saw a long tail-like thing attached behind the uvula. He took a forceps and pulled out a leach about three inches long and a half inch wide. She had lost so much blood that her life was at stake. She eventually recovered, and the family was so thankful. Then he was told by the translator that other children had died apparently from the same problem because of them drinking from the streams. Later Alex had another child from whom he was able to remove a leach, and the child recovered.

Alex had many complex surgical patients. One woman had an ectopic pregnancy of about four months. The fetus was fairly well developed, and the whole mass with the blood was about the size of a volleyball. He was able to do the surgery, and she was recovering. She was followed by a patient with a large thyroid that had to be removed, which was additionally difficult as Alex had to give training to his surgical assistants (in those days they were called "dressers") while the surgery was being performed. But his assistants were quick learners, and he felt God and the angels were with him during each surgery. Then he had an Arab with a broken leg who was so distraught. He did not realize Alex was repairing his broken leg, as before when someone had a broken leg, it would be amputated. He was much relieved that his leg would be made well again. He had another man who came in that he had to remove a portion of the large bowel. It had become twisted, so the blood supply was cut off, and part of it was completely gangrenous. The people came from so far away that it was amazing they were still alive. He was alive after surgery, and we continued to pray he would get well. Another patient came in after a difficult childbirth that caused a terrible fistula. After doing reconstructive surgery, she would be recovering well, but if she had not had the surgery, she would eventually die because of infection.

Now on a happy note. We have just had our first wedding in our chapel. The airplane hangar the king gave us has been made into wards, classrooms, and a lovely chapel. We decorated the chapel with greenery and flowers from our compound plants. They always have a big feast as well. Both bride and groom were hospital workers. Alex gave the groom a white shirt and loaned him his suit to wear. The director of nurses, Helmi, gave the bride a dress to wear, and I made a little white dress for the flower girl to wear. I wish everyone could see the needs of these precious people. The average annual wage was thirty dollars. We helped them with the traditional wedding feast. I made three cakes, and Helmi made cookies as well. Our hospital did not serve meat. The Moslems always expressed their appreciation as they will only eat meat killed by a Moslem. The daily menu is different types of wat made with legumes and served with their injera bread. At weddings they usually serve a cow. We attempted to teach them to not eat raw meat, as the usual was that they would hang up a cow from which the hide had been removed, and the guest will take a small knife and cut off pieces and then dip the bite of meat into a hot spice powder. We had an overseas pastor of another denomination, who came for parasite medicine every few months. Alex had told him that he should not eat raw meat, but he said he liked it and wanted to be the same as the locals. Not a good idea when it comes to that custom. They had several delicious vegetable wat dishes as well as some cooked meat dishes as well.

The big rains were returning, so everyone was harvesting. Part of our mission compound was being harvested. One man will sing out a sentence, and then the eighty or so people who are cutting the grass by hand will answer in chorus. It really is beautiful to hear. The teff grain is probably harvested like in Bible times. The grain is cleaned by the women with huge straw "pans," and the wheat is gathered and ground locally. We saw huge sacks of all kinds of spices. We can understand that the Queen of Sheba took so much spice to King Solomon that probably he had never seen so many varieties!

Patients. We had more patients coming every day. Alex had several patients that had thyroid problems with large goiters. One lady came in for her large goiter to be removed. She did well when he removed the goiter. It weighed two pounds. She recovered well and later married Mamo, a young man who worked for us. Another patient had an ectopic pregnancy that was almost the size of a volleyball that had to be surgically removed. Another lady came in, and there was time to schedule a C-section. The baby was healthy. Another patient was brought in where someone had tried to deliver the baby and had a leather thong tied around its neck. Unfortunately, the baby was dead. Another lady was brought in, and pus was coming out of her; she had had a hard labor that had caused a fistula as well as infection. She survived and was able to have surgery, which was successful. Another young lady was brought in, but her husband would not give permission for surgery. Her pulse was thready and her blood pressure was low. She had lost so much blood, and finally the husband gave permission for surgery. Alex was able to give her a blood transfusion and did the surgery required, and we were so thankful she lived. Another day we had two patients that had to have colostomies but would recover and be repaired later. So sad, a young man had been hit by a truck and was brought in by his father. His leg was full of gangrene, but the father would not let Alex amputate the leg and took him away to die. There was a helicopter crash, but fortunately the pilot was brought to our hospital with only minor injuries. A German man was brought in who had taken poison attempting suicide. It was too late. He could not be saved.

On a happier note, the hospital was now complete. The building was complete after two years. We had sixty patients. It was a real hospital fully equipped, and the patient rooms and wards were completed All the equipment had been installed. How excited we were! Alex could do surgery with a real surgical light above and a real surgical table for the patient. A school had been opened for all the workers. The teacher had completed the seventh grade and was nineteen years old. All the workers began in the first grade. Now we needed more workers.

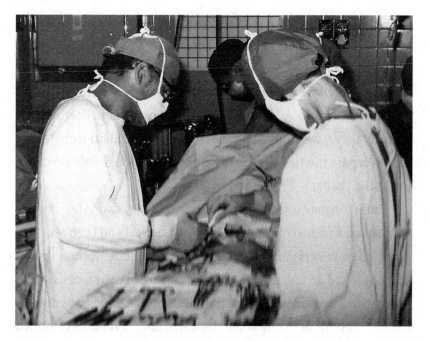

Alex in surgery—Taffari Makonnen Hospital

We had never lost a surgical patient. God had guided Alex's hands. Then one night they brought in a man who had been stabbed ten times. There were ten holes in his abdomen, and his bowels were full of blood. A round worm was sticking out of one of the holes. Unfortunately, he was the first surgical death as he did not survive. At the same time a man came in with tetanus and was able to pull through. Death and life were often seen so close together. We were having heavy rains—two seasons in Ethiopia, the little rains and the big rains. The little rains could be just as heavy. We heard that a woman had been washed down the river a few days ago. We were surrounded by mountain peaks, even though we were on a plateau at eight thousand feet. The heavy rains sometimes cause the mountains to break away. Several people were gathering grass and firewood on the side of the mountain when they were all buried in a mudslide. The rain was also bad for the dangerous roads that wind around the mountains. A bus once rolled over three or four times. They brought our hospital eight patients that had survived the crash. The roads were always a problem. On our last trip to Addis Ababa, we had nine flats. Fortunately, halfway there, we stopped at a prison, and an Italian inmate was able to repair the tires to finish our trip. We bought all new tires in Addis Ababa.

Unfortunately, one night I began to bleed, and Alex knew I was having a miscarriage. He ran to the hospital and then sent two young men to carry me over on a piece of metal attached to two poles. I looked up and saw tears streaming down their faces. At that time, we had an Ethiopian male nurse to help Alex. Alex was doing a D&C to stop the bleeding when the nurse said, "Emete has stopped breathing." (Emete means "Lady," as in Lady Diana, in Amharic. It is a term of respect.) Alex stopped the surgery and gave me artificial respirations until I could breathe on my own. Then he finished the surgery. The next morning when I awoke, the Ethiopian pastor's wife, Wizero Almaz, was sitting by my bed with tears rolling down her cheeks, too. We could not understand each other because she did not speak English, and my Amharic was not so good, but we both understood the language of love! The Lord again manifested His wonderful power, and the next day I was able to get my strength back. Through God's help, Alex had saved my life.

We decided to write to a colleague of Alex's who was an obstetrician, to see if we could adopt a baby. He wrote back that a baby would be ready for adoption in a few months. We were so happy and said that we would take it, boy or girl. Then we got the good news that Alex was invited to the wedding of the sultan in Ascita, for his fourth wife. It would be in May. I had just arranged for our mission station to sponsor a seminar and camp to train our youths in Ethiopia to begin a youth club called Pathfinders. This program was launched by our world church, and we wanted to be a part of this as it was just for youths, and most of our children in Ethiopia could learn so much about living healthfully as well as being taught how to live from Bible principles. We began preparing. I made eleven pints of strawberry jam from the strawberries in our garden, which would help with breakfast muffins. We bought extra wood and lots of legumes to make food. We arranged for the hospital to make injera. We worked hard to get all our youths in the proper uniforms.

Pathfinders at Lake Hyke

A shirt and short pants for the boys would cost one dollar, as our workers at the hospital helped to make them. A lady, Mrs. Bjaarnes, was visiting us and helped to make the girls shirts and skirts. Our mission president, Pastor Axel Varmer from Denmark, supported our project, and thirteen of our mission stations would be sending delegates. We had arranged for a youth leader, Robert Osmussen, to come from Kenya, and all was set. The first night we were to have an "Altar of Fire" where the children could write on bits of paper what they wanted to clean out of their lives. The camp had been planned for May 4–9. Then the dates collided. Alex went to the wedding, and we received word that the baby boy was born, and I was to fly to the States to bring him home. The seminar for the youth program was to begin Friday night, and I would have to fly to the States on Saturday evening. Alex arrived back on Thursday night, and we drove to Addis Ababa to catch the plane on the next day. My good friends Mr. and Mrs. Norman Toews, Australian missionaries from Kuyera, took over the youth program, and all went well.

On the way to the sultan's wedding, the Land Rover thudded and stopped. Hugo, who was a good mechanic, raised the hood and saw that the engine had fallen on the axle. That had also caused the oil pan to leak. Somehow, they got the car running again and continued across the desert road to the wedding. The sultan's wedding was something like out of the Arabian nights.

There were sword dances, camel races and other games, and hundreds of Danakils. Alex recorded all the activities on his Bolex camera. The feast was huge. At the time of the feast, a servant brought Alex a large dish of food. Alex saw that it was different from the others. On the plate was spaghetti, rice, fried potatoes, and bread. There was also a bowl of boiled camel's milk—all white food. He asked the translator why his food was different, and it came back through the two translators: "White food for a white man." Possibly Alex had been the only white man who had ever been a guest of this tribe. They were known as warriors and probably the most feared tribe in Ethiopia. Years later, when the new government of Ethiopia came in, the soldiers came to take the sultan prisoner. He told them if they took him, his people would fight. The soldiers left, and overnight the sultan fled with his family and some warriors over the desert in their Land Rovers to Sudan. The soldiers came back and killed many innocent Danakils at the local market.

When I arrived in the United States, I was able to pick up our precious baby boy, who we named Alex Charles (nicknamed Chuckie). He was a beautiful baby and already active. It had taken a month to receive the letter that he was born and another week before I got there. Alex wanted me to be checked by a doctor because of my problems. Alex's friend, an obstetrician, told me I was eight to twelve weeks pregnant and could not fly. I would have to remain in the States until our baby was born. This was going to be a difficult time, as I had numerous problems. I knew that I had a problem with my blood. It seemed that under stress, my blood would not clot. Alex wrote, "Isn't it something, that maybe we will have two children when we were hoping for at least one!" He understood that with the complications I had, there was a possibility that I would not carry the baby to term. Alex came to the States when I was six and a half months pregnant. He would not leave Ethiopia until a doctor was sent to replace him. Our hospital was staying full of patients. At thirty-two weeks, Joanna Lynn (nicknamed Joni) was born. How we praised the Lord for keeping the baby and me safe! A week later, I survived a severe postpartum hemorrhage. Six weeks later, we returned to Ethiopia with two babies—a girl and a boy.

Alex with Alex Charles (Chuckie) and Joanna Lynn (Joni)

Because of my problems, I would need to give baby Joni formula. How could we do this? The Lord provided a friend from the American Embassy who gave us cases of formula for as long as she would need it!

We returned and resumed our work. Alex had a lady with a ruptured uterus and had to do a hysterectomy. Another older man was obstructed for three days and was delirious. After surgery, he was smiling and had recovered nicely. A man with an infected hand who was bitten by a hyena was given the rabies vaccine. Alex had to operate more bowel resections. Seems there is a time of the year when more obstructions happen. One man was obstructed for eight days and lived. We heard of a child who had been given tapeworm medicine and had died. They make a tea from a kasso tree for getting rid of worms that can be fatal.

Our children's program was expanding. We had 120 one weekend. We had a little party where we served bananas and cookies. We were to have guests from our mission headquarters, so we prepared a special program for them. We had the workers build a ten-foot tukul (the local round type of house) in front of the hospital. Alex made a little platform beside it, and we used a bamboo separator screen behind it. Then we made a huge arch of eucalyptus and flowers in front of the platform. Alex put lights around, as the program would be at sundown and early evening. We had all the children in their new, green Pathfinder uniforms, and thirty-two Helping Hands, thirty-two Friends, and six Companions were invested. All were in the tukul and came out for their parts in the program. Six boys dressed as shepherds (almost all of my children were actual shepherds) and they recited Psalm 23 holding a large picture of Jesus as the shepherd; the next group told of the young people of the Bible; the next group told of their lessons, and all came out on the stage at the end in a huge semicircle and sang "Give Me the Bible." The brethren were all impressed and said they would try to send someone to continue the children's work after we were gone. These years with those children had been so special to us. We taught them, and they became like our own extended family. Shortly after this program, one of my older boys was bitten by a poisonous snake and died. Poisonous snakes do not usually live in our mountains, thankfully. We only saw one snake, which had been run over by a truck and was dead, in all the years we were in Ethiopia.

We decided to send three boys over the last year to our training school near Addis Ababa, where they could learn and come back to Dessie to help us. We sent them Bibles as gifts the first year they were to spend Christmas away from home. We received a precious thank-you note from the oldest boy, who could write English, and he signed it, "Your heavenly son." Two of the boys finished high school and went on to college. The boy with Christian parents became a doctor, and the Moslem boy, who also became a Christian, became an English teacher. The third boy died young. Education is so important to bring health to these people. If only we had the ability to immunize all the children. We too often hear of smallpox and typhus epidemics. Malaria is still the scourge of the lowlands. We were grateful to be living at eight thousand feet with no malaria there.

Good news! Alex was establishing a permanent clinic in Ascita. We were able to buy a European-type dwelling house and the clinic building for $8,000. Unfortunately, we had no budget to take care of the expenses that it would need. Then the examining table was a door on top of four barrels. We needed equipment. Pastor Hugo Palm and Bob Newberg would remodel the buildings for use, as they had been standing empty for a long time. A young nurse, Lydia, and her husband, pastor Solomon Andreas, were chosen so she can hold clinic and he as a pastor and can help the tribe with their problems.

Alex always enjoys these trips to Ascita despite the difficulties! There is always wildlife to see—groups of zebras, ostriches that would run in front of the car (an ostrich fell and seemed so embarrassed), camel caravans, and always something new to see. There was always a problem with the desert road. It was just a trail and difficult to stay on. One time a bridge was washed out that was about halfway to Ascita, so Alex and a helper stayed with an Egyptian fellow who had a house nearby. If they had been on the other side of the river, it would have been days and maybe weeks before they could have come back. They had to give up that trip and return. Ascita itself was a beautiful oasis of flowering trees and all kinds of birds. Unfortunately, the river is muddy and contains crocodiles. On one trip he was able to help a girl who had been bitten in the thigh and was able to get away from the animal. Crocodiles drown their victims and put them in an underwater cave or shelf until the meat spoils. Alex planned to visit about every six weeks except during the season when the roads were impassable. There was no other medical help for this tribe. Mr. Robert Newberg, the laboratory technician in our hospital in Dessie, was able to put a shortwave transmitter between the clinic in Ascita and Dessie, which became a lifesaver. One day he was called to go to Ascita, as malaria was particularly bad. Peter Myheer and several members of the sultan's family were extremely ill. When he arrived, he saw two hundred patients in one day.

One morning we were surprised to see hundreds of men in their national Ethiopian dress carrying rifles coming through the mountains on their way somewhere. Alex looked for someone to tell us what was happening. Then we got a call on our shortwave radio saying, "Do not use your shortwave!" and then it went off the air. We finally found out that these men were ready to go to Addis Ababa and fight for the emperor. There had been an uprising or coup against the king while he was out of the country on a state visit. Evidently when he heard what was happening, he immediately returned to Ethiopia, and the uprising was put down quickly. There was some fighting, and our home for our nurses at our hospital in Addis Ababa had a few bullet holes, but no one was injured.

The children were growing strong and healthy, and I needed help with the laundry. Unfortunately, the lady that came to help had children of her own, and when the children were about six months old, she happened to have chicken pox. The children, of course, got chicken pox but survived well except for trying to scratch their "itches." They never had a cold and were extremely healthy.

After five years of service, our mission allows us a furlough of three months. Amazing we had been in Ethiopia and time had quickly passed. Alex wanted to make one more trip to Ascita before we were to leave. He took two helpers to finally install a pump for the water at the new clinic. The first water pump had been filled with sand. Months later another pump was installed but only brought mud. Finally, the pump would be installed properly, and everyone was excited about taking a shower! Everyone had been covered with sand. Now the water was cool and clear! How nice a cool shower would be! The temperature was 110 degrees in the desert.

He would also see patients. One of his patients was a young boy who had been swimming across the Awash River and was cut across his scrotum by a sharp bottle or rock, and it had to be repaired. Alex had to sew him up without any anesthetic, and the child was very brave! In that tribe it was a shame to cry, and somehow he made it.

After returning, we had a beautiful young Egyptian lady brought in from near Ascita to our hospital. Her husband was working in another area of the desert, and though word had been sent, no one could find him. She was bleeding profusely. Someone had given Alex vacuum transfusion bottles when we first left Seattle. Alex was able to get two units of blood from her abdomen and give it back to her. She had an ectopic pregnancy, and without the blood she may not have been saved. Her husband was found and came to the hospital. He was so relieved and happy that his wife was alive and recovering. The governor of the province had surgery and did well and became a friend. He had told people not to come to our hospital but now was completely changed. Alex also did his second splenectomy. It weighed four pounds. The hospital was full. Alex even wanted to enlarge the hospital with fourteen more beds. Our hospital had fifty-five beds when it was completed.

When furlough time came, Alex decided that he would take further surgical training with all the complicated cases that he had done. We had had a few months to prepare our mission for the new missionary to come. Our garden was flourishing, which would be a great help. Most all the mission work was expanding. Alex had 150 or more coming to adult services, and I had more than two hundred children coming every week. We felt the Lord had really blessed. How sad we felt to be leaving! The hospital workers and our church planned a special evening for us. One of my oldest Pathfinders, Kassahun, spoke at the program. He said, "Before the mission came, we served the god of the evil eye. We were afraid of him, but now we know and serve a God of love that loves each one of us!"

That is why we had come to Ethiopia—to share God's love We

fully planned that we would return to Dessie after our furlough was over, but this was not to be.

The mission needed a surgeon at our hospital in Addis Ababa, and to our surprise that is where we were sent upon our return. Before we left the States to return, a physician gave Alex a child-sized bronchoscope. Our supplies had already been shipped, so Alex put the bronchoscope in his suitcase among his clothes. It had always been the custom that as soon as Alex returned to Ethiopia he would immediately begin work, as there were always patients waiting for him. This time a phone call came from the palace. One of the grandchildren of the emperor was having difficulty breathing. They were told to bring the child in, and Alex examined the child. He then ran to our house and got the bronchoscope. He was then able to use it to take out a jewel that the child had inhaled. The child recovered, and we were again amazed how God provided the exact instrument that was needed to save a life.

Arriving in Addis Ababa, we were provided with a house that looked like it was stucco but had thick walls of mud and straw. We had a large fireplace, and essentially it was the same size of our house in Dessie. The main difference was that we had electricity all day. In Dessie, we had electricity from six o'clock to ten o'clock at night only. We were fortunate that when Alex used the generator doing surgery, we would drop everything and vacuum or use another electrical appliance.

What did Alex find in Addis Ababa? A very old one-hundred-bed hospital with one central, shared bathroom. He talked with all those involved with our hospital, and thankfully they all came to the same conclusion—voting for a new hospital. The mission board agreed. Three years later, we had a modern 140-bed hospital.

Empress Zewditu Memorial Hospital

It probably had the first elevator in the city. Next to our hospital was a new nursing school building, and it was the beginning of a new work for the people there. We had five doctors, and to Alex's great pleasure, we also had our first hospital administrator! No longer would Alex have to unstop toilets or resolve disagreements among the workers. Henry Scoggins was a wonderful businessman and did a tremendous job. We loved his family as well.

What was the purpose to have a new hospital? More people could be served. The new equipment would make the hospital more efficient. We were able to bring in more hospital workers. This was a new day for our medical work in Ethiopia.

We prepared a special celebration for the opening of the new hospital. The emperor himself would share in the dedication program of our hospital. That day will never be forgotten as we saw the new hospital opened. It was a time of thanksgiving and praise to the Lord. Many special guests from the community were there to help us celebrate the opening.

Emperor Haile Selassie with Dr. Bokovoy at the hospital dedication

The patients came, filling the new hospital. One lady who had eight children came and would have to have her leg amputated. The emperor himself came to see if that had to be done. We had the rich and the poor. The rich were charged more to help with the poor. Some resented this, but the local Catholic priest wrote in the newspaper why he felt that this was proper. Our hospital was open to everyone of all faiths or of no faith.

Shortly after our new hospital was opened there was a terrible plane crash at Ethiopia's airport. An East African Airways plane had asked that some dead birds be taken off the runway. This was done. Then the plane was taking off the runway when it hit something that had fallen from a Cessna (a steel jacking pad) on the runway, so the pilot decided to abort the takeoff. The pad had punctured the right-hand nose wheel tire; following this, the no. 1 rear main tire burst. The left outer wing of the aircraft struck a steel lattice tower forming part of the approach lighting, which ruptured the fuel tank and released fuel. The fuel promptly ignited. (This information was obtained from the flight safety foundation, April 18, 1972.) Unfortunately, the plane split in two, with half going over the end of the runway down about thirty feet and the others half remaining on the runway. The plane burst into flames. The passengers were caught between the seats. There were 107 occupants and a total of forty-three fatalities. Apparently sixty-four people were able to get out of the burning plane. Almost all had been burned. They came into the hospital with their clothes and skin in shreds in many cases. it was a terrible sight. It just happened that I was in the hospital at that time waiting for my husband to come home for lunch, as we were having visitors. Alex did not come home and stayed until all the people had been helped. Many were children that were being sent back to boarding schools in Europe. All the passengers were brought to our hospital. Fifteen of the worst burned were sent to Germany, and Alex had to wire one man's face together so he could breathe. The rest were treated by our workers. At the memorial service held in our church by a Lutheran pastor, the pastor said, "When things like this happen, we ask where was God? I cannot answer that, but I can say I saw God at work, with the doctors, the nurses, and all those who helped in the hospital."

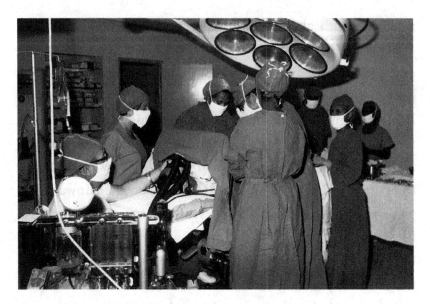

Alex in surgery in the new hospital

At Christmastime, we decided to take our two children to have their pictures taken with the baby lions. The emperor had an area with lions that were taken care of in the middle of town. One of his titles was the Lion of Judah. For one or two dollars, someone would bring out the babies for you to hold. We gave the man some money, and he brought out two adorable lions. They were probably about two months old, and although they looked cute and cuddly, they hissed and spit so that the children were not sure what to do, so the man put the lion cubs beside the children where they were sitting, and though they attempted to pet them, they did not get to hold them.

Chuck and Joni with two-month-old baby lion

We had a special treat once or twice a year—our missionary family would go to Sodere, which was an area with an Olympic-size pool by the Awash River. The pool was fed by natural hot springs. We would take a picnic lunch and spend the day. One day we took a large picnic basket with a lid. Inside I had a large TupperwareTM bowl with a tight lid. In it were our cookies. Chocolate chips were expensive, and so we would make four batches of dough for one six-ounce package of chips. The children looked up and saw that above the pool some monkeys had opened the basket and the Tupperware and were stuffing chocolate chip cookies in as fast as they could. The children ran from the pool, but the monkeys were gone before they could get to our picnic basket.

Joni and Jimmy feeding vervet monkeys at Sodere

The Awash River contained several large crocodiles. We often saw twelve- to fifteen-foot crocodiles. Alex had seen people in Ascita, another area of the Awash River, which had lost hands and legs from the crocodiles. One of our young missionaries from Germany told us that he had been asked to show some tourists around Lake Shala. He oversaw the farm at our Kuyera University. This lake has hundreds of flamingoes. He had gone to this lake often to take tourists, so he thought he would take his bathing suit and towel and take a quick swim while the tourists were walking around this lake. He showed the tourists the path and went back to his car to get his swim trunks. He reached in and got his towel, but his swim trunks were not there. He searched and gave up. He caught up with the tourists and on the way back when they were near the car they could see down in the water into an underwater cave. Six large crocodiles were swimming there at the exact place where he was going to dive in. He thanks God for the angel who hid his swim trunks!

We began our children's program in the capital. We started again with twenty-five and it kept growing until we had 120. Because of malaria, we would not take them camping in the lowlands, but we could go to the forests in the mountains. The area called Metagesha was full of beautiful big trees like the redwood forests of California. High in the tops of the trees were the Colobus monkeys, which are white and black. Unfortunately for them, their skins make beautiful rugs. We were told that a stash of thirty thousand skins had been found by the patrol. It's amazing there are some still flying from tree to tree in the forest today. The hospital provided our wat and injera, and we were able to camp on this mountain. How the children loved the fresh air and the activities provided for them! We also had vacation Bible school every year. It grew until the last one had over 350 children. I led this one in partnership with pastor Girma Damte. This man of God is a dynamic speaker. He translated my teaching into Amharic and captured the children's attention.

Vacation Bible school in Addis Ababa

We were told that an Ethiopian Airlines plane had landed in Addis Ababa. It was December 8, 1972. We were to receive a patient that had been wounded in an attempted hijacking. Seven members of the Eritrean Liberation Front had tried to gain control of the plane. A hand grenade that was armed by one of the hijackers was rolled down the aisle by a passenger. The grenade exploded in the rear part of the fuselage, some six inches off the plane's centerline, blowing a hole in the cabin floor and damaging or severing several controls of the aircraft, including the throttle of two engines, the rudder, and the horizontal stabilizer. The six security guards killed six of the hijackers, and the seventh died at the hospital. One of the men who had been shot fell on a row of three seats, landing on the laps of men from Britain. A senior Tenneco oil company executive was hit. He was brought to our hospital, and Alex worked with him and did the surgery that was needed as shrapnel had hit him in the neck. When he was released to go back to the States, Tenneco paid for Alex to accompany him back to Houston. Alex was so excited to be able to accompany this patient back to America! Later the company gave our hospital a 400-mil amp X-ray, which was more than a $100,000 gift!

Now it was vacation Bible school time again. I think I will retire at forty! There was so much to be done. The rains had stopped, but the weather was very cold. I would have three helpers, but we may have more than two hundred students. We divided them into groups of forty to fifty for their Bible lessons. They were so good though; I know it would be impossible in the States, but there the children were so interested in whatever they were taught. How I love them all!

The emperor would soon be celebrating his birthday. He would be seventy-eight years old, and it was to be a great celebration as it was also his fifty years as king. The city was decorated, and large posters and banners were everywhere. Then Alex and I got an invitation to go to the palace for his celebration. Rose Kennedy was there to share his birthday as it was her birthday also. The day of the celebration I got to meet her at our Italian's salon. She was friendly and wanted her hair to be bouffant, so Ensel, the Italian hairdresser, had to redo her hair until it was "high" enough. That night she was dressed in a white gown with a beautiful white fur stole. She recognized me and stopped as she and her two daughters were going down the red carpet and shook hands with me! Because of Alex's work, we got to meet US visitors through the American Embassy. We were so impressed with one of the presidential candidates, Senator Humphrey, but not so much with Vice President Spiro Agnew.

Again, after being here for five years, we would be going home on a furlough. Alex would work for a few months to bring in some income. We would enjoy seeing our parents and being in wonderful America again.

We left with our little family, flying over the Pole and to our first stop on the West Coast. While there we attended church, and a friend showed us the church bulletin. It said the pastor wanted to know if anyone was interested in adopting a baby. This lady wanted her baby to be adopted in a Christian home. This was not planned, but yes, we were interested, and soon we had a little chubby baby in our arms. We named him James Dean. We were able to pick him up from the hospital when he was one week old. The nurse said, "You won't have trouble with this baby; he just drank a full eight-ounce bottle! "Our older children immediately welcomed him into our family and helped to take care of him. We visited each of our families and enjoyed the time in the United States.

We returned to Ethiopia by flying to Athens, Greece, for a few days so Alex could get over the jet lag; he knew he would be doing surgery as soon as we arrived home. The Lord had blessed us with the family that we had always wanted, but it was a different life with three precious children. We decided to do a little sightseeing and began the trek up to the top of Mars Hill. Chuckie and Joni were playing, but Alex admonished them to stay in the path as the rocks were like marble and very slick on the sides of the path. However, Chuckie stepped off the path and fell and broke his arm. It was the weekend, and the only place we found open was a Red Cross clinic. The doctor asked if we could buy some plaster, but the pharmacy did not have any. However, the Lord must have provided, as the doctor looked around again and found some plaster in one of his hospital coat's pockets and so put Chuckie's arm in a light cast. When we returned to our hospital, Alex X-rayed his arm, and it was in perfect alignment, so he was able to add cast material and strengthen his cast. Two days after we arrived home, we attended a huge potluck by the missionaries after church. Jimmy was now ten months old and had been so healthy, but he apparently picked up some bacteria and became extremely ill with diarrhea and vomiting. Alex called the Ethiopian pediatrician. The doctor told us to give him only electrolytes, which we did. We knew we were joined by all our missionaries in prayer. Hours passed, and finally he showed some signs of life. He took some fluid and was able to keep it down, and finally the worst was past. We thanked the Lord as we watched him as his strength returned. One thing we learned in the mission field is that the Lord is with you wherever you are. How we praised Him!

When Jimmy was three years old, he was eating watermelon and somehow his chair turned over, and his fork went through his tongue, cutting his tongue in two pieces. With the help of Dr. Ted Flaiz, a dentist, Alex was able to stitch it back together. Again, we were afraid it might swell and keep him from breathing, but again he survived. Our American general neighbor supplied him with ice cream from the embassy until he could eat again.

*Jimmy with one of his friends, Enoch, pictured
first as a child and later as adults*

Our children throughout the years were seldom sick. They were healthy and grew so fast it seemed to us. Chuck grew a foot between twelve and fourteen years of age. He was six feet tall when we left Ethiopia. Joni also grew, and we found she needed new clothes. A Lutheran friend heard of our problem. She had just received a large box of girls' outgrown clothes. Her daughter could not use them, so Joni was blessed with a new wardrobe that was almost like new! The children never were bored. They had the Ethiopian children to play with. Chuck played soccer with other students, and Joni by invitation rode her horse at the British Embassy grounds. On the weekend we would go on a short drive; gas was $8 or $9 per gallon. There was a hill covered with oregano, and we called it Pizza Hill. Another hill was covered with semiprecious stones. We often saw wildlife beside the road, and there were many places to hike. The landscape can change from plateau to areas that have waterfalls or rise to extremely high mountains. Our favorite place was in the mountains where the tall redwood-like trees grew, but because of the distance we could only go once or twice a year. The children had dogs and cats, along with other interesting pets, including a one-hundred-pound tortoise, baby deer and goats, pigeons, and Chuckie's adorable pet owl who lived in his tree house.

Chuckie with his pet owl Gugi

In our last term of service, we took a short vacation to Mombasa. We had told the children to beware of the shells; some could kill you. The children took their buckets and spades and went to play in the ocean. Beautiful and unusual fish were in the ocean. Chuckie got the idea that they could catch one. They tried and tried, but the fish were elusive, and then they saw a beautiful "angel" fish going slowly through the water, so Chuckie took off his T-shirt and gave it to Joni so that when he could herd the fish close enough, she could catch it. She saw the fish and put out her hand, which accidentally touched its feathery sharp barb, which immediately stung her. The pain was terrific, and she dropped everything and tried to run to the beach. She came screaming to us and told us about the fish. Alex had a book about ocean fish. When she pointed out the picture of the fish, "the lionfish," it read, "can be fatal." We all got into the car and went to the closest clinic. There they gave her a medicine for severe pain and told us to watch her. There was nothing else to do! Again, we prayed. It was more than six weeks before the swelling left her fingers, hand, and arm. She fully recovered. We thanked the Lord!

It is good to know that every family has its joys and unexpected problems, but life would not be nearly as interesting without those precious children to share it with. Some would hesitate to go to the mission field because of the dangers for their children. Our children changed our lives, and the joys far outweighed the problems. We saw that our children's lives in the mission were rich with unique experiences.

The mission had a one-room school for the children with a teacher from America. Chuck started first grade with Mrs. Rigsby, who had grown up in South Africa. She was the wife of the medical director and was an excellent teacher. Joni went to a German kindergarten. Then the mission brought Miss Fearn Hiten to teach the missionaries' children. Joni began first grade with her and Chuck second grade. They finished all eight grades with her. She, too, was the best teacher they could have had. They took the ninth grade by correspondence and were ready for regular American school. They both made excellent grades. I taught them piano lessons for ten years, and they learned to play. I also taught the local children, but the school had only one piano for practice, so with seventy-two children, a third learned to play, a third learned some, and a third never had a chance. I also taught choir for the school, and they would sing for church. Some Ethiopian children also were attending the mission school. Amharic, the national language, was also taught in the mission school.

The last days of hospital work in Ethiopia were filled as usual with patients. One mother had fed her baby forty days with nothing but rancid butter. The baby was skin and bones. She brought it in for us to save. In the city, the patients could buy their own medicine. One lady had 120 abscesses from injections of pain medications. Another family had carried their sick baby over their heads while going through a river where the bridge had washed out. She was able to be made well again. Traffic was causing a problem especially for the children as only recently were more cars on the roads. One girl had a broken leg, which Alex repaired. A young boy came in with a fractured skull. A piece of bone was sticking out of the occipital part of the brain. Again, Alex had to attend to him and do the needed surgery. He recovered well. The Lord constantly performed miracles, it seemed. Another lady patient came in with a large lipoma on her thigh. She said it began when she was a child. When Alex removed it, it was almost the size of a football and weighed ten pounds.

Again, the news came to us that Peter Myrreh had been in Harar and had a bleeding ulcer. He died before they could get him to medical help. Alex and I had been asked to provide the music for his funeral. It was to be held in our large fifteen-hundred-seat church. On the podium on one side would be the throne for the emperor. In the middle, the casket would be draped with the Norwegian and Ethiopian flags. Hundreds of people were there in mourning. He had given his life for the people of Ethiopia—an unsung hero. It made a deep impression upon us both, and we vowed that wherever the Lord called us, we would work for Him and be faithful to the end.

Ethiopia, with its breathtaking beauty and the wonderful people who had become like family to us, would be forever in our hearts. Now our oldest children were teenagers and ready for academy so we made the decision to return to the States for their education. How difficult to make this decision, but God had more work for us to enjoy.

Family photograph in front of the Empress Zewditu Hospital, just before we left Ethiopia in 1974.

We had been through Europe, on other trips to and from the States. Ethiopia is almost exactly halfway around the world, so we asked if we could return by going the other way around. We rode elephants in Bangkok, visited Singapore with its modern architecture and very old places that have been written about by many authors, stayed at our hospital in Hong Kong, and were treated by former classmates to a miniature vacation. Japan had its gorgeous trees and buildings that had been protected during World War II. So much of the world to see. All of us enjoyed the different ethnic foods. We ate muterbak on a banana leaf; we had noodles of all kinds, and wonderful fruit that we had never heard of before: guavas, rambatans, durian (leave that for the locals), and other tropical fruits. We found people in every country so helpful and kind. We decided there were only a few people in this old world who cause major problems. While visiting Singapore, we were told that they needed a surgeon with British qualifications. Alex, having been born in Alberta, Canada, had taken his Canadian boards so would be able to get reciprocity from Britain. We decided to accept the position in Singapore, since they had Far Eastern Academy where our children could continue school. We returned to the States for a short vacation and then returned to Singapore to work for two more years, which gave us twenty years as foreign missionaries. We will be forever grateful for the full life that the Lord has given us. The needs of the world cry out today. We have seen hospitals that closed because physicians have not been found to continue the work. Pray with us that the Lord will be able to find young workers to fill the positions.

Why Christian missions and missionaries? It literally is to save lives both physically and spiritually. This is a text I received on August 10, 2012, from one of my former Ethiopian girls who now lives in Paris.

How are you Mrs. Bokovoy? It's been a long time since we have met! (about thirty years) I'm happy to get you in FB. I'm happy [that] Joni and you are like my family. I still go to church. I'm getting stronger in Christ day after day [and] you are the one who put the seed of salvation in my life not only me but hundreds of Ethiopian children so today I stand on the side of God don't forget what God has prepared for you! I am very thankful you and your husband God bless you and all your family, Zewditu.

There is no greater joy than service for others! The purpose of this little book is to awaken in the youth a desire to follow our Master no matter when or where He calls. The pastor Robert Moffett from years ago said, "There are a 1,000 fires in Africa that have never heard the name of Jesus." In the Bible in Isaiah 6:8 (KJV) it states: "And I heard the voice of the Lord saying, Whom shall I send, and who will go for us? Then said I, Here am I; send me."

Printed in the United States
by Baker & Taylor Publisher Services